The Tallest Pygmy

The New Paradigm for Transformative IT That Every C-Suite Executive Must Know and Understand

Mark Giannini

KATO BADGER LIMITED
MEMPHIS, TENNESSEE

Published by Kato Badger Limited

Permissions Department
Kato Badger Limited
Kato Mitchell
Post Office Box 341343
Memphis, TN 38138
901-235-2059

Editor: Steve Williford
Cover and Interior Design: Brittney Williford

Library of Congress Cataloging-in-Publication Data
Giannini, Mark
The Tallest Pygmy
ISBN 978-0-615-45108-4
1. Business   I. Title

Printed on acid-free Paper
2 3 4 5 6 7 8 9

Dedication

To my Mom and Dad, who have always been my two biggest cheerleaders! Thanks for everything!

Acknowledgments

I would like to thank my dear friend and editor, Steve Williford, Kelli Mitchell, Dean Proffer, and Megan Majors for all of your help, encouragement and input; Brittney for the great and fun layout; Jeanne Seagle for the illustrations, and especially many thanks to Kato Mitchell and Badger "Goldie" Williams for taking the plunge and publishing my first effort.

Thanks again – it was a fun ride!

THE
Tallest Pygmy

Table of Contents

Introduction

After more than 20 years in Information Technology, serving as trusted adviser to hundreds of successful CEOs, I felt it was time to put some of the lessons learned on paper. Over the years I've seen many trends, heard lots of hype, and witnessed many companies make costly, unnecessary mistakes.

The Tallest Pygmy is my attempt to help the legions of CEOs and senior executives I may never meet by sharing my observations, expertise, and wisdom gleaned in the trenches. I do so in the hope that you won't fall into the same business traps caused by IT departments that cannot, or simply will not, keep abreast of the rapid pace of technological change and innovation.

This book serves as a friendly caution: If you, as a CEO, don't embrace and leverage IT for your competitive advantage, you will find yourself losing more and more deals and clients – and you will not know why.

Far too many times, I have seen organizations that have fallen behind in technology and have suffered severe consequences. Old, poorly functioning equipment leads to critical system failures, lost business, and disgruntled employees unhappy with their work environment because their productivity is hindered.

On the opposite end of the spectrum are organizations that

spend tremendous sums of money on systems and technology that do not benefit the business. I've uncovered numerous situations where the aggregate dollars spent on maintenance contracts alone could be reallocated to replace antiquated equipment with brand new machines that have a three-year warranty.

Talk about waste!

Sadly, I've also seen IT budgets so bloated that hundreds of thousands of dollars could be eliminated and returned to the business without any loss of productivity or functionality.

In many businesses, there's an empire of people whose day-to-day activities and responsibilities are largely unaccounted for – who are not accomplishing goals or producing results aligned with the stated business objectives of the company. In some cases, it adds up to millions of dollars squandered each year. Yet, the CEO keeps funding the budget because he or she has no place to turn for objective advice.

In all of these instances, I find "the tallest pygmy" running the IT department. The reason is that many CEOs are not comfortable or familiar enough with Information Technology to be able to properly assess their IT leader and his or her ability to use technology to transform the business.

There is no shame in lacking this knowledge. The issue here is that if you do not bring in an outside trusted adviser to give you an unbiased opinion on IT strategy – much like you do with your accounting, insurance, and legal functions – then you won't achieve optimal results for your company.

Technology can be a huge transformative agent if properly used to grow and differentiate your business. Not embraced, you put yourself at substantial risk that can potentially cost your company time, money, reputation – and eventually clients.

The Tallest Pygmy is about dysfunctional IT groups within organizations, how they were created, how they hinder organizational growth, and ultimately make the organization less competitive in the marketplace. More importantly, *The Tallest Pygmy* is about what you can do about it.

Let's begin.

Preface

Hello.
If you are reading this book, I'm assuming you have some IT concerns.

So, let's go to the Ocoee River in Tennessee. Its world class rapids were used for the Olympics a few years ago. A ride down it with the High Country Outfitters will cost you about $40. On a recent trip, 40 customers went out on about eight rafts. That's $1,600.

High Country assigned a photographer to take those neat white water photos early in the trip. By the time everyone got back to camp, he had them loaded in a computer ready to be shown on monitors. All you had to tell him was the name of the guide in your boat. A printed large photo was $18. The frame was $22. Most people bought a photo and frame. Some bought several. You could have a disk of all the photos of your raft for $60.

I'm guessing they tripled their revenue. They did this through technology. High Country was able to use technology to increase their business. And if they're smart, they're getting everyone's email addresses and alerting past customers of specials. If they're smart, they are enabling past customers to go online and order more photos.

A simple example of how technology increases business.

So, what about your computer guy?

- **Does he talk in computer speak?**
- **Does he have poor people skills?**
- **Does he say, "We can't!" very often?**
- **Is his job just to keep things running?**
- **Does he ever come up with ideas for how you can use technology to increase revenue?**
- **Does he often ask for a lot of money?**
- **Has he failed to explain how the IT department works?**
- **Does he look at the world as bits and bytes and blinking lights?**
- **Would he have thought about how High Country could make more money?**
- **Is he delivering business results?**
- **Is he a member of your management team?**
- **Does he bring you ideas and concepts that are transformative to the business?**
- **Does he look at the world as how to invest capital in IT to leverage the bottom line on your ROI?**
- **Would you send your head IT guy to your largest client to discuss a strategic IT initiative?**

Okay, maybe one more question. You assemble your management team and say,

> **"I'm going to be gone for the next few days, but the good news is that Bob (the IT Director) is going to be in charge until I get back."**

Does Bob have the people skills, the big picture mentality, and the common sense to be able to do that?

I want to show you how the IT department can (has to) work with you to make and keep customers. Oh yeah, and keep employees.

> **"I want to show you that the IT department should not simply be keeping the lights on, but should be strategically and proactively synergized, giving you a competitive advantage over your competition."**

I'm going to share a few thoughts with you in the course of these pages that should save you a lot of frustration and money. And along the way, I'm going to share some insights to show you how others are using technology.

Mark

Note

We have different learning styles. I learn through stories and examples. I like to hear how a company dealt with tragedy, created success, or fixed a problem. I love the turn of a phrase to explain frustration or triumph.

I have a business partner whose learning preference is very different from mine. She can forego the stories. Just give her the bottom line.

Of course, if I followed her advice completely, this book would be about three pages long. I happen to think I can make much more sense of my concepts and advice by sharing real life examples. Plus, they are worth retelling your staff as you get them on board.

In the event you see the world as my partner does, I have provided The Bottom Line at the end of every chapter. That's probably where you'll want to go. It gives you the main point of the chapter.

1 | What Is a Pygmy?

I was at a college yesterday. One of the administrators said,

"I called the IT group for help resetting a password. Guess how long it took? Three days."

He told me he's developed a "work around," meaning he had an intern who worked for him a few years ago and has moved on to his own career. Whenever this college administrator has a computer problem, he calls this guy instead of the IT department.

As we spoke, the administrator told me all five computers in his department were down. He called the IT Help Desk and was told they would "write him a ticket." When he asked what that meant, he learned it was IT-speak for,

"We'll get to it when we get to it."

Then he called his former intern, who walked him through a few steps to get everything back up. It took less than five minutes.

That's just one of many indications you might have a pygmy in your IT Department. There are many ways to tell if you have a pygmy, and we'll get to that, but first let me explain how pygmies even come to be.

Where Do Pygmies Come From?

Maybe your company started with ten people.

It grew to 50.

Then 150.

How did your head computer person get to be the head computer guy?

Probably because he knew more than the other nine employees back at the start.

His title may have changed to Head of the IT Department, but does he know any more than he used to?

Not really.

Oh, he might know about vendors and some purchasing details, but basically he still doesn't know much more about IT than he did when he started.

It's going to be hard to compete, if that's the case. It's also going to be hard to stay in business.

A Coaching Analogy

We find in a majority of our IT assessments the company is not making good use of IT to make it a competitive advantage. The old IT mentality says 80 percent of the time should be spent keeping the lights on. Twenty percent (usually lower or none) is spent on innovation. That's shoveling sand.

The world is now about innovation. Keeping the lights on can be outsourced.

"Did you know that your internal IT staff typically quits learning the day you hire them?"

Why? They are so caught up with their day-to-day duties that they're not going to spend time, on their own, to pursue their professional development.

That means the organization is falling further and further behind!

Because the IT team doesn't know the new technology, they are going to be ineffective in deciding and implementing new applications and equipment.

If your guys are old "mainframers," they are led to make a decision in their world of comfort and not in your company's benefit. New and better ideas often don't fit comfortably into their skill set.

So, it would seem better to have a team of knowledgeable IT advisers instead of one, two, or even a dozen people so busy keeping the IT department afloat, they haven't been able to stay abreast of the incredible options and benefits out there.

It's Similar to the Levels of Coaching Baseball:

- **Level One:** You've got the dad who is a volunteer for his son's summer little league team. He's a coach because he has a kid on the team and wants the best for his son. He's not the world's most knowledgeable baseball coach, but then again, he doesn't claim to be, and he doesn't have to be.

- **Level Two:** Then you've got the competitive summer baseball team coach. This is moving it up a notch. This is a coach for players with a future. This team is more serious. It plays more games. The coach is paid. More is required and expected of this coach. He works a little harder on recruitment and who plays what position.

- **Level Three:** Next, you go to the coach of a high school team. This coach should be more gifted and skilled than the previous two coaches. Some of his players will go on to play college.

They practice almost every day during the season, rain or shine. The players are older, the umpires are better, and the college scouts are more interested. This coach works hard on development and strategy.

- **Level Four:** The college-level coach is often better than the high school coach. If he's at a Division One college, he's on salary just to coach baseball. The level of competition is higher. Players are on scholarship. There are more fans. He has a staff and requires accountability of his players.

- **Level Five:** Then there's a minor league coach who is now in the business of baseball. His players might go to The Show one day, and he is expected to provide the training and experience to cause that to happen. His staff is composed of professional coaches. His job is to develop players to their maximum potential while thousands of fans pay to watch.

- **Level Six:** The major league coach is at the top of the food chain of baseball coaches. It is an incredible opportunity, with multiple demands, expectations and rewards. He should be the cream of the crop. The very best. His job is simple. To win. Win ballgames. Win the division. Win the World Series.

You need to look at your CIO and IT people the way you look at this progression of baseball coaches. How did the person you've got come to be?

Often, it goes back to being the tallest pygmy. The company was small, and he was there. The CEO explains:

> **"All of a sudden, we had some computer problems, and this guy liked computers, so we put him on the project."**

It just evolves from there. In many cases, it's not a strategic plan. You didn't hire that guy to be in that position. You've gone from five computers to 200 computers . . . or 2,000 computers.

But you never changed the coach . . .

Ouch.

You've got a major league team being coached by someone who is clearly not a major league coach.

When an organization grows, you have to find employees with skill sets to match the company's size.

"The truth of the matter is that a fast growing company probably has outgrown the skill set of the original CIO."

These dysfunctional coaches are what I call pygmies. Here are a few pygmies you might recognize.

The Stuck Door

Bob's not going anywhere. He's also not helping a whole lot. Not much gets in. Not much changes. He's comfortable with what he does, he's making enough money, and he's never going to leave. Meanwhile, his skills continue to degrade and grow less relevant. He doesn't know how to leverage technology to transform the business.

The Revolving Door

Let's take a different head computer person. He started with you, but he wanted to learn. You sent him to seminars. You encouraged him to learn on line.

And he did learn. And grew. He kept up, understood the big picture and used it to help the company stay competitive. He was eager. Things were perfect.

And then one day, he walked into your office and told you about this wonderful job offer he received.

And he left.

You paid for his education.

And guess what?

He just left with it.

He came. He learned. He left.

You were his training ground. This cycle can happen again and again. You never progress because you are continuing to reset to square one.

Dr. No

This is the entire culture of an IT department that practically says no before you even ask the question.

Sometimes he hates people as much as he loves power.

NO

14

"Can you move this monitor to the second floor?"

"Nope."

"Why not?"

"It just can't be done."

"And you're absolutely sure?"

"No way, no how."

"Okay, because we are having a Board of Directors meeting and they wanted to hear about how the IT department is doing."

(Pause)

"Let me check. I think we might be able to move some things around."

The commonality between Dr. No and the Stuck Door is that neither wants to innovate. They're not thinking about moving things forward. They're thinking about gathering power.

White Noise

I had lunch today with a CEO of a large company who was telling me her CIO has great conversational skills and good ideas. She doesn't mind taking him to meet clients. She said,

"He gets their situation, but nothing happens! It's all talk. We meet and we talk and nothing ever gets done. It's like all this white noise."

15

He's the guy who can tell you who won the 1920 World Series and what the statistics were for each player, but can't pick up a bat and hit the ball to save his life.

A pygmy can actually be well liked and respected, but doesn't make anything happen. (I've described many more types of pygmies in the Value Add Section in the back of the book.)

"That's really the whole thing about pygmies. IT has to innovate, and pygmies get in the way. They don't help drive innovation – probably because they don't know how."

Back to Bob

As I mentioned, Bob was first in charge of the computer department because when your company was smaller he knew more than anyone else about computers. How? He was the tallest pygmy.

We work with companies who are often frustrated by their IT departments. The CEO says,

"Times are tough, and we're cutting line items in every department except IT because they tell me I can't cut any from their budget. And I have no idea why!"

Often because IT is covering itself. It is preserving itself. The CEO doesn't understand enough about the area to implement checks and balances. There is no audit.

A Different Score Card

Sometimes people think head count in the IT department is the key, but by leveraging all the tools available today, you can actually get more done with fewer people.

> **"In the old days, one IT person could support 25 users.**
>
> **Today, using modern tools, that same IT person can support 150 users and 470 monthly service requests.**
>
> **In world class organizations, one IT person can support 800 users!"**

Many IT directors don't need to budget for more people. They need to budget for tools that can transform the department to do more with less.

So maybe you're saying about now,

> **"Wait a minute! Then why do I have so many IT employees?"**

Exactly.

The problem is you have no idea what they're doing. And you have a department which is hyper-inefficient.

It's often due to a pygmy running unchecked.

CHAPTER ONE
The Bottom Line

Maybe you think you have a problem but aren't sure and don't know what to do about it. Maybe you know you have a problem but don't know what to do about it. And maybe you wonder if fellow CEOs have the same problem you have.

- Is your IT department implementing best practices?

- Are you leveraging your IT resources in the most effective manner?

- Does your IT team per-
  haps need help and not
  even realize it?

These are all questions to
ask your IT department.

When you're dealing with
a pygmy, you need confirma-
tion. You need an independent
evaluation.

That's why it's a good idea
to pick up the phone and talk
about it with someone like me.

18

2 | IT – Your Competitive Edge?

W hat finally prompted me to write this book is the fast speed at which technology is moving. It's impacting companies and the customers they serve. That means IT has to be part of the strategic plan. IT must be a part of the strategic management team. IT must help you go to market and sell your product or service faster. If IT is not helping you develop a competitive edge, you are heading for disaster.

I have seen it far too many times.

I don't want it to happen to you.

IT. It's always been this mysterious locked room in the corner. A lot of people coming in and out. Lots of blinking lights. Lots of strange words.

If you're like many CEOs, you've resigned yourself to the fact that IT is a necessary evil. You're going to have to deal with it. You grudgingly write the check for the budget. While you are able to make cuts in the other departments, you are told there is absolutely no place to cut the IT budget.

I have been living in IT departments as an outside resource for over 20 years. I have seen tens of thousands of departments and hundreds of thousands of employees. I have had the pleasure of working with some of the finest IT professionals in the industry.

In the following pages, you'll find some valuable information from my years of being battered around data centers, computer rooms, wiring closets, and cabinets behind the kitchen with servers stacked up in every possible manner. I've worked in pristine data centers. I've also worked in shockingly horrific, carved out pits.

I have spent a significant amount of time dealing with pygmies. These are people who are holding their company hostage. They are not putting the needs and goals of the company above their own.

IT or Firefighter?

You know what the problem is? Many companies think of IT as a firefighter unit. You know, the Tech Unit is positioned in the ambulance, with defibrillators in hand, waiting for the next emergency. This is a model in which your organization is kept alive only through the expertise and wisdom of the IT paramedics.

They respond to Code Red, and then they keep you on life support. Did you get that? You. They arrived just in time. At least that's what they want you to think.

In between emergencies, they maintain equipment and software, perform maintenance, and replace servers and hard drives.

Here's what else we know about what they do. They spend money.

Here's what they contribute, in this model, to your competitive advantage.

Nothing.

As a matter of fact, they are probably not even in those meetings.

The point here is a question.

"Is your IT department proactive or reactive?"

Are they actively managing your network in such a way that they catch problems before they happen?

Do they effectively prevent you from having any down time?

Are they constantly doing the daily, weekly, monthly, and annual maintenance?

Are they looking for ways to enhance the customer experience? If not, you're falling further and further behind.

Think about eating pizza every night and wondering why you never lose any weight. "It's going to be OK," you tell yourself. But it's not. You have to take proactive steps. In order to remain healthy and lose weight, you have to work at it every day.

The same is true with IT. You have to work at it every day. You can't just buy it, set it, and forget it. You can't get so reactive to the emergencies that you are not constantly seeking to be proactive and innovative.

IT as Partners

Compare that with an IT department that is actively engaged in making you money. There's a model for you!

They are active partners in soliciting and maintaining customers. They understand the big picture. They understand your service or product and are consistently looking for ways to give you a competitive advantage.

They are not in the business of saying no, but the business of making customer experiences the very best they can be.

They are actually asking and listening to internal and external customers, and they're making suggestions for new product applications.

Cases in Point

Here are some examples of building systems that were used to a competitive advantage:

- **Online package tracking**
- **Capability to pick up a DVD from a redbox and return it the next day without ever having to go into a video store.**
- **Downloading books to a Kindle, giving you virtual access to a bookstore without having to leave the beach.**
- **Emails detailing the status of your package delivery.**
- **Immediately streaming a movie to your computer or TV.**
- **Designing your own Nike shoe online.**

Unfortunately, companies don't realize that even if they are leading their competitors today, they might be getting further and further behind. If they are standing still technology-wise, they are setting themselves up to lose.

That's how FedEx crushed UPS and DHL. UPS was bigger, stronger, faster, privately held, and more recognizable. They had been in the shipping game far longer.

FedEx beat them primarily because of technology.

They asked and answered questions before UPS.

- **How do you overnight a package anywhere in the country?**
- **Anywhere in the world?**

- **How do you track it?**

- **How do you make it easy to ship it?**

FedEx adopted and leveraged technology to a competitive edge. That is how they differentiated themselves from good companies. Technology helped FedEx become great.

Of course, technology is a two-edged sword. It can be the competitive edge that causes you to compete and defeat larger organizations. However, if you don't get control of it, it can put you out of business.

> **"If you let your systems get very far behind, you are behind in the marketplace."**

Regardless of whether you're in the dry goods business, the manufacturing industry, or the transportation sector, someone is going to come along with a software application that is much more advantageous to your customers, and you're going to be gone.

That competitor with the new technology application, which is driven by IT, is going to allow for more productivity with fewer people for less money. The competitor looks very appealing, while you look like three-day old pizza.

IT, unlike any other department, spans every inch of your enterprise, from the reception desk to the shipping dock, and all points in between. IT knows more about every department than any other department knows.

By having that global view of an enterprise, IT stands in the absolute best position to offer innovative ideas that can help the company grow, go to market faster, and better serve clients.

Freestylin'

Other applications continue to amaze me. For example, Coca Cola got its IT department together with their Research and Development department to create a machine called Freestyle.

This allows one machine to dispense every beverage that Coca Cola makes, including Coke, Fanta, energy drinks, flavored waters, and more. It does not contain cans or bottles. It mixes each product a customer orders.

The Press Release states:

> **"Instead of large, five-gallon bags of pre-mixed syrup, the Freestyle PurePour system uses ultra-concentrated 46-ounce cartridges to mix drinks and allow for a greater array of flavors, all coming from one spout. There are also RFID tags to keep track of all the different flavors held inside the cabinet and their current status."**

And like any piece of 21st-century equipment, the Freestyle has the ability to send back all sort of data metrics to Coke HQ, including what the popular flavors were, when and how much people were buying, and what locations were most favorable. Coke HQ even has a kill switch for any flavors they need to stop offering ASAP.

Machines are popping up in California, Georgia, and Utah, and there will be 60 of them across the United States by the end of summer. The only downside to this thing is that it doesn't let you mix up mind-bending suicide cocktails, like a Peach-Grape Fanta with a touch of Sprite. One can only hope.

What an active role IT is playing! They are no longer in the background.

IT has typically been passive. They sit around, waiting for problems to happen. And they fix them. They're waiting to be called off the bench, instead of already being an aggressive player in the game.

Customer Involvement

Front-runner companies want their IT departments to be involved with the customers.

So, let me ask you this question. When is the last time your IT department was at your customer's place of business?

Would you encourage that?

Would you be terrified to see that happen?

The reality is probably yes.

But wouldn't it be a win-win for your IT guys to be looking at your customers' businesses, asking, "What can we do to help?"

How can we help this customer with its website to help them sell more of our product?

We want to get you up to speed so that you're better, stronger and faster. And we can also show you how to sell more of our product.

If you look back in history, it's not anything new. Look at American Airlines a few decades ago. Before the days of customer-driven computer travel, they put computers (the Sabre network) in travel agents' offices to enable them to communicate better with American Airlines.

In doing so, they enabled travel agents to check flight availability without having to call the airlines – something customers couldn't do. This increased travel agents' business. It also increased American Airlines' business. It was a win-win situation.

American Airlines gained market share through its IT department. The sophisticated technology made it easier to do business and it also did something else. It strengthened the umbilical cord. It was harder to unplug.

IT departments help their customers do business easier, and also make it less appealing to disengage. IT can transform the way you do business.

Using Technology to Make the Sale

This past winter was brutal in Memphis. During one particular cold spell, my pool was partially frozen and all the tiles came off, which necessitated me getting them all replaced.

During this time, I decided to check my Viking Grill, and I found some of the parts had rusted and were in disrepair.

I'm not a very mechanical type person, but I am motivated by saving money. Because I had spent so much money getting the pool fixed and had already made an investment in the grill, I thought, "Surely there is a kit to refurbish the grill."

I couldn't be the only guy on earth with this issue.

So, where do I go? (This is the critical question for all customers.)

The Yellow Pages? Nope. Never use them.

Directory Assistance? Nope.

The Viking Store? Nope.

A grill store? Nope.

I went online and searched for "Viking" and the model number.

I eventually found a website called GuyBanks.com. Guy Banks represented himself as a purveyor of fine cooking equipment. He had a "renew kit" for Viking Grills. It was all the parts and pieces

I needed simply based on my model number. So, I purchased it. When I got the box, I found the grills, grates, brackets, burners, screws, and instructions. It was everything I needed, and I saved about $500 by buying them separately.

Now, I would have paid the $500 extra just to know the parts were all there and I didn't have to buy everything separately. I'm the kind of guy who would buy the wrong part and would have to send it back. The whole process would have taken months and would have been a whole lot of trouble.

Guy Banks has identified the Viking customers who bought pretty expensive grills, and made the refurbishing experience quick and easy. He took a group of items and turned them into a kit that even I could assemble. What a great idea!

So, now that I have refurbished my grill, I proudly point this out to my friends. Guess what they say? Their Viking grills are in the same shape. I bet I've sold 15 of these kits. Each kit cost $750.

Through technology, Guy Banks has made multiple sales that I'm aware of over his competitors. How valuable is technology? In this case, over $11,000.

What the Future Holds for Us

IT is going to look a lot different in only a few short years. We need to understand that and use that information to our advantage. For example, in the next five years or less:

- **Over a third of businesses will own no IT assets.**

- **Internet marketing will be the predominant way of advertising.**

- **The world will be using hand held devices to do everything a computer once did.**

What's In It For You?

Technology applications can equal more money for your business.

"IT is much more than just maintaining the business. It's about increasing the business."

So, what if a pygmy is running your IT? You're going to make the wrong business decisions because you never knew about a decision that needed to be made. You had a guy who was not thinking strategically.

Technology for Grass

Let's look at a smaller example. Let's say you're in the lawn/ landscaping business. Every week or so, you call your customer (when you catch them), agree on a time, have the customer leave you a check under the doormat (if they remember), and then schedule your guys to cut the yard (often on short notice). Oh, and don't forget to deposit the check (which takes a day or two to clear).

What if you took care of all of that on the front end? When the customer signed up, you determined what would be done, when it would be done and how much it would cost. You arranged for the money to be electronically added to your account on a certain day.

Now you can schedule your employees, not waste time chasing customers (but instead look for more customers), and enjoy timely deposits with immediate access to the money.

An automatic electronic reminder is sent to each customer, reminding them about the upcoming appointment, in case they need to unlock a gate or clean something up.

And how about a web page where customers can contact you about special needs (which immediately reaches your phone), or where potential customers can read about you? You also have the ability to communicate to every customer at the click of a button, "I'm having a special on fertilizer this week and wanted you to know about it."

By using these simple computer applications, customers get better service, and you have the ability to save money and time.

If you look at any business, or any problem, there is always a solution created by technology. It's about customer convenience, it creates a wow factor, and it makes more money.

Technology Promotes Customer Loyalty

Take a look at online banking. When you check your account on your computer, you aren't tying up a bank employee, you're not tying up a phone line, and you're doing the work yourself.

You're accessing information you want when you want it.

Same thing goes for Pay at the Pump. This has reduced the number of employees needed. And it's made it faster for customers. Just swipe your credit card, and you're ready. You don't have to walk inside a convenience center and do business with someone who seems to always be on the phone.

Quicker and easier.

Technology can solve a variety of business questions.

If you're a car dealer, you no longer have to wait on customers to contact you about service.

Through use of a database application, you can send a note that says:

"Mr. Giannini,

Good morning! It is now time for your regular service visit. We have made an appointment for you at 12:00 on April 21. We value your business and are proud of our customer lounge, complete with fruit, drinks, bagels, donuts, and cookies. Your regular servicing appointment is absolutely free. We just need you to confirm your appointment time. If your appointment lasts longer than 30 minutes, we'll supply you with a new loaner at your convenience."

That promotes customer loyalty. It also generates other business and new car sales. And it helps provide the wow factor.

The other day I received an email from a dealer I have used in the past. It said:

"We haven't seen you in awhile. We're guessing you've put another 5,000 miles on your car. We'd love to service your vehicle for you. We included a coupon for an oil change when you come see us. Our records show that it's also been 15,000 miles since you got new tires. We'll be happy to rotate them and let you know how they're doing.

We'd also like to show you a few of our latest model cars and the features they can provide you. At the bottom of the page, you can see how your car compares and contrasts with other

cars. We are offering some great trade in deals right now, especially on your year and model car.

Also, as our way of saying thanks, when you come see us, we'd like to give you a free wash."

I did click through, looked at the new cars, the features, the coupons and brought it to work with me.

The point is we often lose customers and we don't know where they went. We gain new ones but we don't know where the old ones went.

Now, that was pretty easy for them. But think pre-technology. Think what would have been required. They would have had to print thousands of letters, pay for postage, get someone to stuff the envelopes, type the addresses and they still wouldn't be able to personalize it to the customer.

It's expensive and not as effective as the electronic version.

That's someone leveraging technology.

It's a Whole New Ballgame for Success

I was at a friend's house not long ago, and his three daughters were all communicating, but they weren't talking on the phone. They were texting and Facebooking and instant messaging.

These are your consumers and labor pool in five years. If you think you can keep things the same, you're fooling yourself. People buy the way they want to buy. Not the way you want to sell.

"The way you sold ten years ago is not the way people are buying now. If you don't modify the way you go to market, someone else will."

And you'll lose market share and possibly your business. I hear from our clients,

"I don't think our customers want to buy online."

Well, they may not want to buy online now, but they will sometime in the future.

If you're not driving something to enhance customer experiences – something to generate a profit center, something to change the business – you're hurting, and maybe you don't even realize it.

If IT is simply helping you keep the lights on, you're losing money. And market share. And customers. And maybe, again, you don't even know it.

The inefficiency of using people instead of electronic processes shows up when and in what ways you go to market.

If I want to buy shoes, I use Google. I don't have to go to the Yellow Pages. The next generation will not use the Yellow Pages.

If I want sushi, I only have to type "sushi" in my GPS, and it starts telling me all the nearby sushi restaurants and how far away they are.

When I want to go to a restaurant, I go to websites to find customer reviews. I can use my phone's GPS to plot out the destination.

Now, check this out. This is where it really gets cool. I'm a restaurant owner or employee. I just received an email saying,

"Mark Giannini just plotted a route to get to your restaurant."

I then arrange for the potential customer to receive an email or text saying,

"Thanks for thinking about us. Just present this on your phone and receive ten percent off your meal and a free appetizer."

That's what great organizations are doing.
How do you get ahead? One way is to ask,

"What kind of game changing technology can we introduce to make doing business with us extremely advantageous and easy?"

Look at what Netflix did to their competitors, like Blockbuster. If you remember, in Blockbuster's model, you went to a retail store, rented a DVD, drove home, watched it, drove back to the store, and returned it.

Then there's the dreaded late fee. You know what I'm talking about. You forget about it, then you can't find it. Then you find it about the time you get a nasty postcard reminding you about your indiscretion. When you finally take it back, you realize you could have bought the DVD for what you paid in late fees. I understand that many Blockbuster franchises made more on late fees than rentals.

In the Netflix model, from the comfort of your home, you pick a movie with your remote control, hit "Download," and you're watching ten seconds later. No trips to the store. No late fees. Instant movies!

Netflix thrived and Blockbuster sank. The key component for both was technology. Why did you begin to choose Netflix over Blockbuster? Because it was easier.

Of course, that kind of technology is tremendous for the customer because we don't have to go anywhere, but look at what it does for Netflix. Using this technology, they don't have to use a disc, or the mail, or a person.

Guess what's driving all that? Huge servers and lots of bandwidth. Technology.

The idea is the same for every company. Somewhere in the background is a server or servers.

Take Kindle.

Look at the old model. If you needed a book, you found a bookstore – presenting some problems if you wanted to buy a book after the store was closed or if you were in a locale without a good bookstore. Of course, it's also sometimes inconvenient to get in your car and travel to a bookstore. They also may not have the book you want.

Another alternative was to buy a book from a place like Amazon.com. You still had to wait a few days, depending on how much you wanted to pay for shipping, which was extra. If you wanted the book immediately, you were out of luck.

With the Kindle model, you can purchase a book without leaving your home or vacation spot. You get it instantly. No shipping fee. And it's never out of stock.

So Kindle created a game changer through technology to make things easier for the customer. What's behind it?

Technology.

CHAPTER TWO

The Bottom Line

Your IT department is either going to sink or save you. You need an IT department to keep systems functioning and to back up data correctly. You also need IT to improve your organization from operations to sales.

Almost every best practice these days includes an IT component. Our IT audit includes evaluating how well you're incorporating IT to be efficient and profitable.

Any size business should hold a strategic planning session to determine how technology can increase business. It should also determine how technology can increase the value and appreciation of the customer's experience with the company.

How can you make it easier to do business with you?

3 | A New Paradigm

E veryone gets it when the organization loses its largest customer.

They go to the customer and ask,

> **"Why did you leave us? We've always delivered on time, been fair with you, cared about you, and communicated with you. So why, after all these years, did you leave?"**

The customer says,

> **"Well, you've been doing things the same way all these years. It's been fine, but someone just showed us a dramatically different way of doing business that had a major impact on the way we serve our customer. We've been loyal to you for 15 years. Shame on you for not showing us this first!"**

In other words, a new competitor emerged and created a new paradigm so compelling the customer had to go with them.

The "all about me" way of doing business doesn't work. Folks are winning business and gaining market share when they say,

> **"Okay, our competitors are equally good, but the thing differentiating us is these tools. I'm going to help you use them, and they're going to double your business. Yes, you'll buy from me, but you'll also benefit from my accessibility and advice."**

So, no longer do IT service companies show up at potential customers' places of business and tell them about their awards.

The customer doesn't want to hear how great you are.

The customer wants to know what you can do to help their business be better.

Things We Cannot Live Without Today

iPod	GPS
Wii	Smartphones
TiVo	Mp3
Netbooks	Netflix
USB drives	E-Book readers like Kindle

Things We Couldn't Live Without 10 Years Ago

Webcams	Blank CD's
Rechargeable batteries	PDA's
3 ½-inch floppy discs	Film cameras
Analog display	Incandescent lightbulbs
CD Walkmans	Camcorders

Things We Won't Be Able to Live Without in 10 Years

Gesture Technology – Remote-less TV

Proform Trainer – Android-powered treadmill

WiFi Power Outlets – Turn on or off household items from a PC or iPhone

Sanyo's Electric Bicycle

Sony 3D TV

Self-Heating Packaging – Reheat a can of soup on a wireless charging station

Wireless kitchen appliances – connect wirelessly to recipe sites and can adjust heat based on recipe

LG Smart Refrigerator – keeps track of frequently used items and expiration dates

Xbox Kinect – you and your voice control the game

A New Paradigm for Consumers

The successful organization is not just looking at business today, but also at sales trends in three to five years. The customer of today is not going to be the customer of ten years from now. Things continue to change very fast because of technology. So, it makes sense to address new sales patterns with technology.

It's seldom that you see kids listening to a radio in the car. They're not even listening to CDs. They are listening to the iPod connected to their sound system. One iPod holds more songs than every CD and cassette you and your friends ever owned.

Folks watch the news on their computers.

When is the last time you used a pay phone?

More and more people don't have a land line phone. Do you remember beepers? Remember the large cell phones with small coverage areas?

People communicate by voice, texts, tweets, Facebook, and Skype while walking through malls and sitting at red lights.

I organized an event for clients last week, and we didn't even talk via phones. We used Facebook.

Paper boarding passes will soon be extinct. They're being loaded on our cell phones, with readable bar codes – convenient for the customer and money-saving for Delta.

Speaking of airports, take a look at what folks are doing in the terminal. Texting, talking on their phones, and using the Wi-Fi for their computers.

Remember when you had a map in the glove compartment and pulled over at gas stations to ask for directions? Now you just consult the GPS in your car or phone.

As I write this, the iPad didn't even exist eight months ago. Now they've sold four million of them!

Things happen fast.

So, let me ask you a question. Who in your organization is thinking about what's new?

My point is things are changing – rapidly. And we better get ready. We have to look in the looking glass and make some educated guesses for what that consumer is going to want three to five years from now.

> **"The Pygmy is going to say, 'It's worked for the past 20 years. It will work just fine for twenty more.' But there's a new paradigm, and you need to adjust."**

How important is that? Ask Blockbuster.

This can be scary stuff. It can mean business failure. If you don't get this paradigm and its importance, your business potentially won't be around too much longer.

A Paradigm for Employee Quality of Life

Have you ever thought about the fact that IT contributes to employee satisfaction or dissatisfaction? Ever thought that it might even lead to employee turnover? Here's an interesting activity. Why not informally ask ten employees today how computer-related activities contribute to their quality of life at work.

Then follow that up by asking if the IT department's level of support adds to or subtracts from their quality of life in the workplace.

What's good for the external customer is also good for the internal customer. It's a new paradigm for them too. Part of being a successful organization is the ability to attract and maintain great employees.

I recently read an article that claimed over 50 percent of all employees are on the lookout for another job. That's a huge shift from the last generation, when folks stayed with one company all their working lives.

So, why do employees choose one workplace over another?

Pay? Sure.

Convenience? Sometimes.

Leadership? Absolutely.

Corporate Culture? Yes.

Safety? Certainly.

Recognition? Often.

What about quality of life within the workplace? I know that includes many things. It might mean free and accessible parking. It might mean good benefits. It might mean good food in the cafeteria. And it definitely means user-friendly IT applications and support.

Can you think of any piece of equipment the majority of employees use more than their computers and computer applications? What happens when computer applications fail? In many arenas, work stops, revenues go down and tensions rise.

What happens when the IT department is incompetent or adversarial or both? The same thing. Quality of life comes into play. I'm suggesting that a poorly run IT department can add to your employees' job dissatisfaction and contribute to your turnover.

Like I said, it's a whole new paradigm out there.

IT applications should be held to the highest standards. If CIOs can't produce, they should be ushered out the door.

While visiting a client this week, I was talking to the CEO's secretary who said,

"Let me ask you a question. When I send an email with an attachment, how long should that take?"

42

I told her, depending on the size, a second or two, at most.

"Oh. So if I push "Send," go get a cup of coffee, and it's still showing the hourglass, that's too long?"
"Yeah. I would say even if the coffee pot was on your desk, that's too long."

As a matter of fact, I would send emails with attachments and the CEO wouldn't get them. I would send them to her and she wouldn't get them.

They have problems.

The big problem is they don't know where to turn.

An entire organization just accepts that it takes a long time to send emails and that they sometimes don't receive attachments at all.

Think about the productivity loss for 40 people. Think about their level of frustration. Think about how that frustration level builds and bleeds over into other things.

Here's the even bigger problem. Everybody knows. They don't even go to the IT department. They get it done without them. They wait for the CEO to do something, but the CEO doesn't know exactly what to do, so he doesn't do anything.

Quality of life for employees is a big deal. IT can be the determining factor. That's why it's so important to go to that third party like me and ask questions like, "Is it normal for an email to take this long?"

It Doesn't Have to Take a Long Time to Move Quickly

Here's are some questions for you . . .

- **Have you ever wanted to get something done quickly only to be told by IT that it can't be done quickly?**

- **Have you been told it will take a long time to secure a piece of equipment?**

- **Have you ever been told that the reason for a computer application delay is because it's so complicated?**

- **Have you ever been told there's nothing you can cut from the IT budget?**

Think about getting something new as it relates to technology within your organization. Maybe it's a new server infrastructure. Maybe it's a new piece of software.

We're talking about a business outcome which involves hardware and software to give the CEO the result he wants. Maybe he wants to see trending on the products, which could include cost of raw materials, profitability margins, and market pricing.

In these cases, the owner wants it done overnight. But IT says it will be six months. Neither is realistic, but you can structure an environment to do things rapidly.

Consider the Automobile

Let's compare it to cars. Whether they are expensive or inexpensive, they are all basically the same.

They all have four tires.

They all have doors.

They all have windows.

And engines.

And a steering wheel.

Does that mean that a Toyota shares all the traits with a Lamborghini? Of course not. But there are more similarities than differences.

So, for someone who just needs to go back and forth to the grocery store and has no penchant for styles in automobiles, a Ford Taurus is perfectly adequate.

Maybe someone has a lot of passenger needs, with plenty of room for luggage, or bicycles, or strollers. Then it's a Suburban or a Minivan. There's nothing fancy about running carpool. You just need a lot of space.

The same is true for IT. It doesn't always have to be the best to get the job done. When you look at IT systems, the basic infrastructure is very much like cars. While every system is different, the platform is pretty much the same.

Take a commodities firm, for example. There are a lot of email transactions. There are a lot of complexities. There are buys and sells and calls and puts. There is a lot of modeling. There are a lot of triggers that automatically buy and sell at certain price points.

But even with a very sophisticated IT department, the basics are the same, making it easier to build an infrastructure you can expand upon quickly.

IT departments are often not keeping abreast of new options out there. So they make it more complicated than they have to. More importantly, they don't really know about regular upgrades. They only upgrade when something breaks. Now you're in fire-fighting mode. At that point, there's no plan.

> **"Uh-oh! We've got a hundred people not working because this thing just bit the dust. Call the computer guy and tell him to get the first server he can find. Whatever it is will be better than our seven-year-old model. Just get over here fast!"**

There was no one to offer a master plan involving a little more room for consolidation.

A third party like me could have said,

> **"Instead of having these 15 servers, we're going to have one big server and put everyone on it. This will save money and hassle. It's afford-able, it's manageable, and it's easy to maintain. Also, we can at last design a workable disaster recovery plan."**

The Future Answer

The IT department in the future for most mid-size companies might surprise you. It will be outsourced.

I was with a client two days ago who kept lamenting its small IT budget. They had a critical failure that caused them to be down for three days. The CEO said he thought there had to be a better way, and he did not mind spending more money to fix the prob-lem.

I asked him to let me take a look at his budget. Honestly, I thought he would have to spend more money.

Here's what I found. They were spending money on the per-sonnel responsible for this failure. They were spending money on maintenance contracts they didn't use. They were overspending on equipment. They were buying licensing for things they didn't need.

So, they were spending a lot of money for a result that wasn't getting the job done. The answer was to outsource.

We ended up taking their existing budget and giving them brand new equipment on every desktop. Everybody got a new 24-inch monitor. We are now hosting their servers, and we cut their monthly IT budget by $3,000. So now, every three years, they are going to get all brand new equipment. They have zero IT worries and instead of the couple of people they had on staff, they have our entire team to support them.

CHAPTER THREE

The Bottom Line

An IT service company doesn't show up at potential customer's place of business and talk about its awards. That way of doing business doesn't work anymore. Folks are winning business and gaining market share when they say, "Okay, our competitors are equally good, but the thing differentiating us is these tools. I'm going to help you use them, and they're going to double your business. Yes, you'll buy from me, but you'll also benefit from my accessibility and advice."

The successful organization is not just looking at business today, but also at sales trends in ten years. Today's customer is not going to be the customer of ten years from now. Things continue to change fast due to technology, so it makes sense to address new sales patterns with technology.

Things are changing, and we better get ready. We have to make some educated guesses about what that consumer is going to want a decade from now.

The pygmy is going to say, "It's worked for the past 20 years. It will work just fine for 20 more."

But there's a new paradigm, and you need to adjust. For many companies, outsourcing of IT is the way to go.

4 | Social Media – Free, Free, Free!

I
T is not going away. If it hasn't already, it will become your most powerful tool. Are you leveraging it effectively?

I am on the board the Dixon Gallery and Gardens. We had a new fundraiser this year. It was a bonfire event called Art on Fire. Since this was our first year and we had a limited marketing budget, I simply posted a note about it on my Facebook page to my 4,000 friends. I drove awareness to the event. If half of those friends reposted it, that's 2,000 posts. How many collective friends did those 2,000 have? I don't know, but I have heard of many people who went to the event because they heard about it through these alerts. It drove excitement, and that excitement built attendance.

It took about a minute, and thousands of people saw it. If 50 people actually went because of reading this post/re-post, and each spent $75, that's $3,750 the Dixon received.

Not bad for a minute.

So many companies simply do not take advantage of social media such as Facebook, Twitter, etc. Why not?

Good question.

Twitter helps businesses engage with customers locally and globally. And, by the way, inexpensively. But also effectively.

49

That's a great combination – inexpensive and effective.

Facebook allows you to build momentum. It helps get the word out quickly for your business. I also use Facebook for the nonprofit causes I'm involved in. For example, last year, when I was involved in a project for the Girls and Boys Club, I created one post that became 500 messages. If those folks forwarded my message to a few others, I touched about 2,500 people – in just a few minutes.

Think about the difference between that and sending 500 letters. Think of the time and expense and trouble.

A meeting took place this week at a local private high school. The new development officer greeted the faculty for the first time. He immediately got their attention when he said,

> **"We're no longer going to be asking faculty for donations to the school. I'm not interested in you contributing your money to the school. What I do want to ask you to do will have a far greater reward for the school."**

He then encouraged the faculty members to go to the school's website and add some positive comments to the Feedback section. He pointed out that thousands of alumni read the website each week. He said the alumni like to keep up with what's happening at their alma mater, and the faculty could affect good will and possible future endowments, simply by writing a few positive words about what's going on at school.

That takes very little time – no envelopes or stamps – and has the potential for a big payoff for the school. That's the magic of a social network.

The Wave

Social media can be used in a variety of methods. We call one of the methods "The Wave." That's where every member of the group posts a message at a particular time. For example, for the Boys and Girls Club Steak and Burger fundraiser, I would post something for Steak and Burger between 8 and 9 a.m. Someone else would post something between 9 and 10. And on it goes.

By only eight people posting in a sequence to people who are going to repost to their friends (who repost to their friends), we calculated we touched at least 250,000 people! It was free, fast, and effective.

It helps people in your community feel like everywhere they turn, they hear the same message. Suddenly, you go from being nowhere to being everywhere.

It particularly helps small corporations communicate to large numbers of people at no cost.

But it's free, and everybody's out there. It's how we stay connected and reconnected. You just have to learn how to harness it.

As a matter of fact, I've even received messages in these arenas that say, "Hey it's good to hear from you again. I now own a business and I need your help."

Social media isn't just for people to talk. It's also for doing business. And if your business is not out there . . . it shows.

By not using social media, you're missing out on touching your consumers of tomorrow. Remember, they have never picked up the Yellow Pages. They don't subscribe to the newspaper. They read fewer magazines. They read more and more electronic media.

They are not watching TV the way their parents did. Most of what they watch is prerecorded, which allows them to digitally fast forward or eliminate commercials.

And they live on sites like Facebook and Twitter.

What Is Your Purpose?

IT's purpose is not to support the business, but to drive the business.

The problem is that they are analyzing data instead of looking for new ways to use it for a true competitive advantage. The key difference in IT in the future will be its ability to drive technology to help the customer.

So, maybe it starts by asking your IT department to reinvent itself. How do they respond when you ask the question,

"What is your purpose?"

The correct answer is,

"We grow the business."

In good times, CEOs have let IT departments get by. They thought of them as a necessary evil and expense. Now, CEOS are saying,

> **"Wait a minute! I'm spending a lot of money on IT. But I'm not really getting anything other than someone to keep the lights on."**

Keeping the lights on is important. But for the amount of money spent, there should also be major innovation going on.

As I've said, the day an IT person is hired is typically the day he or she quits learning. They take off the strategic thinking hat and replace it with the tactical firefighting helmet.

"If you're fighting fires, there's no room for vision."

If that's all you do, after a while, all you do is think about shoveling sand. You forget about the number one purpose of your business – your customers.

Facebook Got Me an Employee

I'm a big fan of Facebook. I use it more and more every day. Let me share a few ways I've used it this past week.

I used Facebook this week to advertise a job opening we had here at Service Assurance. We had over ten people apply for the position.

As it turns out, we hired someone very quickly. It was a woman who had applied for a position a year ago. Although she was not selected for the job, she became a "friend" through Facebook. When she saw the post, she immediately applied, came in for an interview and was hired.

Consider the "old school" alternative. We would have had to put an ad in the paper, wait until Sunday for it to run, lose training time with a current employee who has to leave soon, and spend money.

If we had used Monster.com, we would have paid hundreds of dollars and received resumes from strangers from all over the country.

Facebook, on the other hand, was quick, free, and led me to folks I knew, or who knew my Facebook friends, who had recommended they submit an application.

How I Met Harold Collins

I ate lunch with a friend the other day. I asked him his thoughts on the ten people, in Memphis, who were doing the most good. He shared his list. Turns out I knew most of the people already. Until he mentioned Harold Collins.

Harold is the chairman of the Memphis City Council. I did not know him. But I went to Facebook and found Harold. I saw that we had about 60 mutual friends.

So, instead of trying to track his number down and leaving a phone message, I sent Harold a message through Facebook. I wrote:

> **"Dear Mr. Collins,**
>
> **I was eating lunch with Larry Jensen, a mutual friend, and he spoke very highly of you. Considering our similar visions for the community, he was surprised we didn't know each other. I would like to see if I could buy you lunch and listen to your thoughts on how to make Memphis a better place."**

Three hours later, I received a response, and we scheduled a meeting.

There's a lot of power in that. He could go to my Facebook page and see who I was, what I did for a living, and what I did for the community. (You can go there, too.) That's been a great way to meet people I want to meet. If you're a CEO and not on Facebook, I urge you to join. If you look at my profile, I have few photos – I don't publish every vacation and activity.

I link newspaper articles that my company has been featured

in. But I mostly use Facebook to promote the charitable work I'm involved in.

It's the new and improved version of the cold call. You've got a picture. Your story is told.

I can't think of anyone I've reached out to on Facebook who hasn't responded favorably. I'm talking about reaching out legitimately. Not to make a sale but to simply meet to talk about how to make Memphis a better place.

Facebook is a great way to break the ice. It's noninvasive, and it helps you build your professional network.

Will some of those meetings result in business? Yes. But it's more about forming relationships. Business will follow.

Groupon

There's an organization on Facebook called Groupon which means Group Coupon. It's a service offered nationwide. The one I subscribe to is in Memphis. The subscription is free.

Groupon offers a special every day. Some days, I'm interested. Some days, I'm not.

Well, this week, I saw a Groupon for a bicycle "basic tune up" for $40 from Midtown Bike Company. I have a bicycle that has been in my barn for the last two years. It needs to be tuned up. They're going to oil it, grease it, make sure it's in great condition, then wash it.

Midtown Bike wanted to get the word out about their shop, but they wanted the coupon to be controlled. They didn't want a mad stampede to their place of business. If they had an ad in a newspaper, they would have no control.

But through Groupon, they could limit the number of coupons they want to redeem. The Groupons can stop any time Midtown

Bike wants to stop them. And I will use the printed Groupon as my payment.

It is probably a break-even proposition, but it gives the customers a chance to learn who Midtown Bike is.

When I printed my groupon, it said,

> **"Because Midtown Bike has had such an overwhelming response, this Groupon will not be valid for one week."**

They could control when people came in to redeem their Groupons. I noticed today the Groupon was half off on a haircut at a particular barbershop, between 1 p.m. and 4 p.m. – probably a slow time. They're not overloading during peak time.

It's all made possible by technology. And the expense of advertising was nothing.

Interim Restaurant

Today, I was wondering where I was going to eat lunch. No big deal. I think about that all the time. I was meeting some clients over near a building in Memphis called Clark Tower. There are many places to eat over there.

I chose Interim. I chose it because I received an email from the restaurant with its daily specials. One was something I really like – a grilled pimento cheese sandwich. Now Interim is not cheap, but this sandwich was only $6.

When I met the three other people, we kicked around lunch ideas, and I suggested Interim. As it turned out, they ordered more expensive items, and our bill was about $60. Not a bad return on an email that was free to send out.

An Opportunity for Someone – Right Now

Right now it's 3:00 in the afternoon. I'm thinking about dinner. Being single, I know what I have in my refrigerator. Nothing. I ate out the last couple of nights. So, if someone sent me an email right now, whether it's a pizza place, a steak joint, or an Italian eatery, maybe with a photo of the special, I'd consider it.

It's a gorgeous Tuesday afternoon. A restaurant could send me an email that says,

> **"It's such a pretty day – we'd love to have you come join us on the patio. We'll pay for dessert."**

I'm probably there.

Or my local grocery store could send an email saying,

> **"It's a beautiful day out! Why don't you enjoy some Great King Cotton hot dogs over the grill?"**

It would make me want to do it.

It's free, it's easy, and it can be triggered at the drop of a hat.

Dominos Pizza

Dominos is now in the online information age.

I recently ordered a Dominos Pizza. Soon after, I got a text that said,

> **"Louis is now making your pizza."**

About three minutes later . . .

> **"Louis just put your pizza in the oven. It will be out, piping hot, in 12 minutes."**

Six minutes later . . .

> **"We just spun your pizza around in our 825-degree patented convection oven, and it's looking good!"**

Six minutes later . . .

> **"Louis just took your pizza out of the oven and has placed it in a box. Joe has loaded it up and is on his way to your house. Get ready for the best pizza you've ever had! He should be there in seven minutes."**

Technology models allow them to know how long it will take. About five minutes later, you receive . . .

> **"Joe should be getting close. Sometimes you run into traffic, but he's on his way!"**

Five minutes later, he's at my door.

Compare that with the all-too-often horror stories of pizzas that never arrive with no communication from the pizza place.

Now, did someone at Dominos Pizza watch Louis and Joe and type me a special message? No. It was all predictive models. But they stayed in touch. And kept me updated. I didn't have to wonder.

They probably also had a way of saying things were a little slow and it was going to take a little longer to receive my pizza.

As Kemmons Wilson, founder of Holiday Inn, used to say, the best surprise is no surprise. I can accept my pizza being a little late. I just don't like to be kept in the dark about it.

A little later, I received an email asking how the pizza was. If I respond, I get some electronic coupons for my next order.

Or, through technology, they can in essence say, Mark usually orders a Coke with his pizza. He didn't this time. Let's give him a free Coke next time. Let's see if we can get him back in the habit of ordering a drink with his pizza.

Every business, including yours, should be using (and can be using) technology to get more customers and make your cash register ring.

CHAPTER FOUR

The Bottom Line

Your business should be using (and can be using) technology to get more customers and make your cash register ring.

Facebook is not just for people to talk about their children and hobbies. It's also for doing business. If your business is not out there . . . it shows. By not using social media, you're missing out on something free, and you're not touching your consumers of tomorrow.

The younger generation is making their buying decisions online. Remember, they have never picked up the Yellow Pages. They don't subscribe to the newspaper. They are not watching TV the way their parents did. They live on sites like Facebook and Twitter.

When is the last time you've had an executive session on How We Can Leverage IT to Grow Our Business?

What does your website look like? Does it encourage commerce? Or is it an aging afterthought?

5 | Murphy Will Sooner or Later Find You

I t's amazing to me how many companies are leaving themselves open to disaster. Along with best practices in leveraging technology, other best practices also have to be observed.

Most companies aren't following best practices in data protection. They are blindly moving along, thinking,

"It won't happen to me."

Now, it doesn't matter what type of customer satisfaction you've achieved if your data goes away. That's what I have seen many times. You have a company that is productive and growing. Well, all of a sudden, it has a critical event – the sprinkler system comes on, the building burns, the floor above the IT department has a toilet overflow on a Saturday and no one sees it until Monday – and all your stuff is gone.

Speaking of Backup Horror Stories . . .

I'm living one right now. The next few pages show that not all IT related disasters are the result of water, fire, or heat.

We were brought in to help a banking organization. They have a CFO and a "computer guy." He is very smart. A wiz bang. But...he doesn't know what he doesn't know. He is unconsciously incompetent. Very dangerous.

This gentlemen set up a machine to back up emails. It's an important part of any organization, especially where government regulations are involved. He also bought software for the backup.

The machine he bought was the right one to buy. The software is what I would have suggested. The server he used was a good Exchange server. The hardware was configured correctly, complete with redundant drives.

So what's the problem?

He didn't set up the software correctly. So, while he thought he was getting a backup, he wasn't.

That was problem number one.

Problem number two was he never tested it. Ever. Because he was the genius.

The backup was never getting done. Not only was he not getting a backup, but he also didn't know when a drive was failing because he didn't set that part up either.

One drive had failed for three months! And just yesterday, the other drive failed.

Things could have been salvaged at this point, but the computer guy didn't know what he didn't know. So he tried to restore the backup to the failed machine. He continued doing the wrong things until he wrote over the existing backup, leaving the organization with no emails or email contacts for the last three months.

They have no email history and no email currently. They will not be able to get the old email back, and they won't be up and running for another couple of days.

They've engaged us to make sure this never happens again.

Here's the hard truth about this event. The computer guy

needs to go. I don't know if he will or not. For the same money the organization is paying him, our team can ensure that the IT is running efficiently, is tested regularly, and is backed up religiously.

An incompetent computer employee can do a lot of damage. Maybe you think you're saving money by using him, but you're really not. Reputable, certified technicians not only identify and fix the problem faster, but can also directly talk to the manufacturer.

The internal computer guy had no clue what to do.

He was like me when I tried to paint my own kitchen. When I finished, it looked like a 3-year-old had done it. I had paint all over the hardwood floor. I had kicked the bucket over, almost fallen off the ladder. And, of course, I had to hire a professional to fix my mess.

While Computer Guy may have loved putting all that stuff together, he had no clue about the business consequences that were about to happen because of his ignorance.

"That's the problem with the internal guys. Many sit in their caves, with their massive walls around them. This group is not friendly to the internal customers."

Do you know what they're doing back there? They're playing World of Witchcraft, they're buying things on eBay, they're answering Facebook, and they're reading your emails.

Ten years ago, if you lost data, you had it somewhere in a filing cabinet, and you could hire a bunch of temps to re-key it.

These days, we don't have filing cabinets. We have document imaging servers. So everything we get paper-wise is scanned and entered into our electronic system.

Combine that with electronic invoices, purchase orders, emails, critical documents. If the system it's stored in dies, you've lost it all. You've lost the original, the source, and system it was processed through. There's nothing to recover. There's no paper.

People assume that's not going to happen. There's not a disaster recovery plan. They don't test their backups.

I often ask a new client,

> **"Tell me how you back up."**
> **"Well, I back up to this tape?"**
> **"Where do you put the tape after it's backed up?"**
> **"I put it in this box."**
> **"What box?"**
> **"That one right there. The one that's on top of the server."**

Okay. So you back up on tape. You put it in the box that's two feet away, in the same room. What happens if your building burns?

Or they show me a safe where the tape is stored.

> **"This prevents us from damage or loss in case of a fire."**

Well, two fallacies.

First, the rating for the safe is for paper. In other words, you may understand the fire can rage for four hours, and the paper inside the safe won't burn. Paper will start to discolor at 180 degrees. And once you get above that, it will combust. But we're talking about a tape. A tape will start to melt at 130 degrees. So the tape is ruined at well before the 180 degree mark.

The other fallacy is that just because it's in a fireproof safe doesn't mean it's recoverable. If the entire building burns, and it's a big building, that fireproof safe is going to be like every other hunk of metal inside the building. It's black. The fire marshall won't let you get it anyway, but even if you could, as we learned in the catastrophe of 9/11, you'll never find it.

If you could find and open it, you'd only find a melted glob of plastic.

Sometimes I hear a little different variation:

"I keep the tape(s) in my purse/briefcase."

Could I see it? And you know how dirty either one is – dust, crackers, mints, lint, gum, and all kinds of things. It gets hot. It can melt, just like your old videotapes you left in your car too long.

Speaking of those videotapes, when you play them over and over, what happens? The sound and video quality get worse and they sooner or later break.

The same thing happens to a backup tape. It uses the exact same technology. Plastic film has a life of about 100 hours. Some companies have been using the same tape for years!

I have seen this practice used by both small and large organizations. They're not thinking and planning and practicing for worst case scenarios.

Catastrophes happen. You need to be prepared.

Question:

"How often do you test your backups?"

Have you ever restored just a single text file or a single email or a deleted document from backup? Are your backups your only solution for disaster recovery?

Incredibly, most companies still back up their system with the antiquated tapes, just like they did in the fifties.

That's why my company doesn't sell tape drives. It's just too simple to use electronic backup techniques to offsite locations. It's called Enterprise data backup and Automatic Data Protection.

Hours or Minutes to Recovery?

While the major disasters are not as common, there are many daily, smaller scale disasters. For example, the CEO has stored and lost his PowerPoint presentation for a big meeting. He didn't actually lose the PowerPoint. He just can't find it. Actually, what he did was save it by the wrong name – his son's resume.

Let's say the CEO saved the file to the tape picked up and he delivered, every day, to a secure location.

Once he realizes his mistake, the storage company promises to have the tape back within four hours. (Hopefully they have not brought the wrong tape, which happens occasionally.) So now you have your tape.

Now a computer specialist has to mount those tapes to find the file. It's sequential. It's attached to two rolls. The tape has to be moved until the file is found and restored. Best case scenario, if you lost a file at 8 a.m., you have it back by 2 p.m. Slow.

Then there's something called the backup window, which means you back up when no one else is on the system. This can take over 12 hours, plus it just doesn't work for all organizations.

In essence, you never catch up. There's just not enough time.

If you had it backed up to disk, it would be much faster. It would be just like looking at your computer screen. You could just open up the file. It would take more like five minutes. That's definitely the way to go.

You can also back up a lot more on disk than tape.

Disk is fast. Tape is slow.

Ask your CIO why you're still backing up by tape. Allow me to make a prediction: Your CIO will say one of three things:

- **Because you didn't want to spend any more money.**

- **Because we already have the tape.**

- **Because that's the way we've always done it, and it works just fine.**

The problem is he's not thinking outside the box. So, here are some questions to ask your IT guys:

- **How old is your Disaster Recovery Plan?**

- **What is your Plan B, C and D?**

What is the Cost of NOT Doing Business?

You know what's incredible to me? That some CEOs have been brainwashed by their CIOs into thinking some downtime is okay. They use that play just like a mulligan in golf.

> **"Bob, we've had our email running for two years without a hiccup, and now it's been down for two days. That's just the way it is, sometimes. "**

"Well, I have news for you. "

"You should never go down. Properly engineered and architected solutions will make your systems bullet proof so that you never have unscheduled downtime."

The problem is most internal IT folks don't think it's a reasonable investment and don't know how to do it.

So, here's my next question: How much does it cost to have 100 people just sitting there, not able to do anything because your system is down? And, by the way, the customer is not able to access your network either.

So, what's that customer going to do? If they can't get what they need from you, they're going to the guy who's next up to bat.

Every customer has a guy on deck. The guy on deck has been told, "I don't need you right now. We're happy where we are. But if anything goes wrong, you're my first call."

Downtime is not okay. It's suicide. The customer is going to buy from the vendor whose computer isn't down. If the service is good, they probably won't come back to you. Why should they?

So let's take a look at what being down just cost you.

Cost of 100 unproductive employees

$$
\begin{array}{r}
100 \text{ employees} \\
\$15/\text{hr salary} \\
\text{x} \quad 5 \text{ hrs} \\
\hline
\$7,500
\end{array}
$$

Revenue loss of a customer(s) who ordered from you weekly

$$
\begin{array}{r}
5 \text{ widgets} \\
\$75/\text{widget} \\
\text{x} \quad 52 \text{ weeks} \\
\hline
\$19,500 \text{ a year}
\end{array}
$$

In total, that's more than $25,000 from just one customer and one period of down time!

Third Party Peace of Mind

Many IT departments are like a traffic cop. One of them has a crush on some female employee, so he's reading her emails. They're looking at the CEO's emails.

A computer company had a commercial a few years ago. It was about hacking, but it makes the point. One guy is asking if the other guy knew that Joe was making $10,000 more than him. Then you see him entering the ENTER key with the words, Everyone knows now!

Here's how the conversation in the IT department goes:

> **"Did you know Mr. Brown is on Match.Com?"**
> **"Did you know Mr. Brown spent two hours looking for fly fishing equipment?"**
> **"Did you know Mr. Brown just sent a resume to Delta?"**
> **"Did you know Mr. Brown has a girlfriend? Check out this email."**

The point is many IT departments can read everything you have – all your emails, all your Internet traffic – and have collected information they shouldn't have. And some disgruntled IT employees have distributed this information with a click of the mouse.

How is the CEO going to know about this? Is the IT department going to tell him?

I don't think so.

We will. And we do.

Let's say you're a smaller company. Why use a third party like mine?

The reason you employ a team instead of an individual goes

back to those earlier two factors: depth and breadth of experience.

A third party team also has the resources that the computer guy just doesn't have and never will have. We are able to go to the senior level technical support at Microsoft, Hewlett Packard, Dell, Cisco, etc. A single person doesn't have that type of ability or authorization.

And what about continuing professional education?

I've spent hundreds of thousands of dollars for my employees to go to the manufacturer to learn their best practices.

Not All IT People Are Like This

I can't end this chapter without saying there are very good, competent, strategic-thinking IT departments out there. I just wish they weren't in the minority. For example, the IT department at FedEx is all about process improvement. It continues to ask,

**"What can we do differently? How can we
make things better for the customer?"**

Process improvement and strategic thinking, that's how.

You used to check your deliveries online. You had to go to the Fedex website, type in your package number and find out if your package had been delivered.

Thanks to the FedEx IT crew, you can now have a verification email or text sent to you every stage of the delivery process. All you have to do is check your messages.

CHAPTER FIVE

The Bottom Line

I have news for you. Computer systems should never go down. Our cost-effective implementations will make your system bullet proof so that it never goes down.

Downtime is not okay. It's suicide. The customer is going to buy from the vendor whose computer is not down. If the service is good, they probably won't go back to you. Why should they?

You should think about outsourcing because you employ a team, not an individual. It's all about depth and breadth of experience.

A third party team has the resources a lone computer guy just doesn't have and never will have. We are able to go to the senior level technical support at Microsoft, Hewlett Packard, Dell, Cisco, etc. A single person doesn't have that type of ability or authorization.

And what about continuing professional education?

I've spent hundreds of thousands of dollars for my employees to go to the manufacturer to be taught their best practices.

Do you have a disaster recovery plan? How about a backup plan?

Have your plans ever been assessed by someone else?

What would happen to your company if your data just went away?

6 | Why Have We Been Successful?

Technology is moving incredibly fast. It's impacting companies and the customers they serve. There is a huge need for more efficient and strategic IT. Over the last 20 years, my organization has helped thousands of companies save money and make money.

I've been asked many times why my company has grown like it has.

"The bottom line for why we've been successful is we've helped our customers be more successful."

How?

A crucial part of it is conducting a baseline assessment. We can't help you until we know what you have and what you need.

If you've ever purchased a used car, you might have taken it to your trusted mechanic before you bought it and said, "Mike, I trust you. Tell me what you think."

That's what we do. We're the mechanic. What do you really need from your mechanic? An expert to give you an informed and objective assessment.

That's exactly what we do. Every business regularly needs a check up for their network status. You need an informed and objective assessment. Diagnosis without examination is malpractice.

Then we create a document with a tremendous amount of information about your network. It's a good reference guide you can hand to any technical person as a user's manual.

Some of our clients want this done every year. They think they know how things are going, but they still want the check up to make sure. So every year, we give an assessment that might say,

"Your network is in tip top shape. You've got great leadership in your department. Here's what's changed in the industry in the last year that you may want to look at. We can make the upgrades for you, or your department is capable of making the changes internally."

Here's what the CEO gets out of this. He knows his department head is good. He knows his network is solid and well protected. It's recoverable in the event of a disaster. We are effectively doing a performance review.

We also sit in on goal setting meetings with the CEO and the IT chief. We assist in helping them reach their goals. Here's the interesting part. Sometimes this is all we do – an assessment and sitting in the goal setting meeting. These businesses actually have a relationship with one of our competitors who does everything else for them.

But they want an independent, third party review, similar to a financial audit. The important part is our objectivity. If it's good, it's good. So we have no trouble giving good reviews to our competition.

You Really Do Get What You Pay For

In the computer business, there's the reputable, legitimate, trained, certified support organization. And then there's the person who offers the cheapest rates in town. He has no industry certifications. He has no access to the manufacturer or senior level support. He often cannot do the type of diagnosis he needs to. And that leads to malpractice, not to mention a lot of damage. In the industry, he's known as a Trunk Slammer.

In our industry, these independents who have no office and work from their vehicles are called Trunk Slammers.

He has persuaded some folks he knows what he's talking about, and he has some customers. The problem is most of these guys know just enough to be dangerous. He's found a few things that work, but neither you nor he know for how long or if that's really the best solution.

Some Trunk Slammers have been laid off work. They have no other options. They don't plan on being in business too long. They have mouths to feed. And while I respect and understand that part of it, the problem is clients are left hanging once the Trunk Slammer moves on.

A Trunk Slammer also used

to be a college kid. Now it's the high school kid who can fix many things. It may soon be junior high.

That's when we are contacted. Trunk Slammers teach organizations a few hard lessons.

While a Trunk Slammer tends to charge less than competitors, he tends to take much longer. Is it worth it to be out of operation for a day? Usually not. You get what you pay for.

True professionals usually take far less time and have an entire organization behind them.

A Trunk Slammer is not as accessible as larger IT service providers. If he's working on one client, he can't come see you until he's finished with what he's doing. More down time for you. In Memphis, we get a lot of electrical storms during the summer. The Trunk Slammer can only be in one place at a time. He can't get to his clients for hours or days. That's simply unacceptable.

You get what you pay for.

Slow response time, slow work, trial and error, etc. And by the way, what do you do when he goes on vacation?

The scariest part of a Trunk Slammer is that he doesn't know what he doesn't know. Some call this "Unconscious Incompetence." Then he hits "Yes" when he should have hit "No," and your entire system is gone. There's no quick fix to that one. Sometimes it's gone forever.

Trunk Slammers burn out. They have no depth. If they have three client problems at the same time, who gets serviced?

Again, if they charge $50 an hour for four hours (and you're not sure what they did – neither are they!), while we charge more per hour and fix it in one hour (knowing what we did), not only did you save money using us, but you also received productivity out of that computer(s) for an extra three hours.

Are you using one of these pygmies?

A Trunk Slammer Horror Story

We see these stories almost every day. Certainly every week.

The client is almost sheepish when they call us in to fix a Trunk Slammer problem. We don't want them to feel that way. We just want to help.

We had a client this week with an email server problem. The Trunk Slammer thought he knew how to fix it. And he did know about 70 percent of the solution. Then he got lost.

The worst thing you can do when you're lost is to throw rocks at the problem. What does that mean?

> **"Hmm. That didn't work. Let's try this.**
> **Okay, that didn't work. Let's try this."**

Ultimately, you throw one rock too many, and you destroy the thing.

This happens because the Trunk Slammers have no one to call. They can't call Microsoft because they are not authorized. They are no different from any other person out there.

> **"They typically Google. This is scary. This is not confidence-inspiring."**

Do you see the picture? You have a large organization and this guy Googling to find out how to fix the problem!

This company does business with clients through email, so who knows what the inactivity is costing. And this guy is throwing rocks. He finally tries something he shouldn't have.

He enters some commands from something he read on the Internet and it erases everything.

There are no mulligans in this game.

It destroyed the email server.

How many orders were lost?

How much information was lost?

How many clients were lost?

How much time does it take to restore all the information?

That's very bad news.

The good news is he'll never use a Trunk Slammer again.

He'll use us – an organization with engineers who help with urgent issues, an organization that can work as a team. No one person is ever going to know the answer to every problem. But most of the time, someone on the team does.

Plus, we have access to the manufacturer, because we have gone through a lot of training and certification. That's why there are teams in business.

Trunk Slammers have no life line. They have no safety net. Unfortunately, clients don't know this. They don't realize the risk they are taking. The Trunk Slammer is the tallest pygmy! He doesn't operate under best practices. All he is trying to do is to make a living.

I can't fault him for that. But he's in way over his head.

"The simple fact is IT doesn't just run on its own. It's like a garden. You have to take care of it daily, weekly, monthly, and annually to keep it flourishing."

I have had Trunk Slammers come to us with servers in pieces in a cardboard box! They are at their wit's end. They don't know what to do.

The other thing about Trunk Slammers is the Law of Diminishing Returns. The Trunk Slammer is thinking, "I'm going to fix computers, and I'm going to get paid to pay the bills."

The problem is there is much more to do.

They have to do the back end work sometime – billing, ordering, marketing, returning phone calls, paying bills, responding to emergency calls. As a one man show, he simply can't do it all. And the more business he gets, the more behind he gets.

It's the difference between value and cost.

Trunk Slammers deliver no value.

Do you want something good, fast or cheap?

Pick two.

You can't have them all.

The Trunk Slammer stories are all the same. They get in over their heads technically, and they can't find a way out. So, they throw rocks until disaster strikes.

We actually give a "What to Look For in a Third Party IT Provider" document to our prospective clients and say, "Use this as a checklist. Talk to our competition. Use this scale on them as well as us."

What to Look For in a Third Party IT Provider.

A live person on the phone.

This is important. Simple? Yes. But I like to talk to another person. So do our customers. Problems are often easier to deal with when sorted out with another human being. I don't want our customers speaking to a recording. I don't want them trying to figure out which prompt to push, which category to choose, and then having to wait for someone to get back to them. I want to be accessible and to make it easy for you to do business with us.

Look for a company that's been in business at least ten years.

Don't trust your business to a start-up. Look for someone who's been in business for at least ten years and is Microsoft Certified. Why is that important? Because Microsoft is the dominant provider. If the provider is not a Microsoft Gold Provider, don't talk to them – they don't value their business enough to put in the time and study to be the best at their game. You need a company with stability. To be a stable company these days, you have to be the best at what you do.

Vendor management.

We help our customers manage all their vendor relationships. So, when it comes time to renew long distance, cell phone and Internet connectivity, we can help. We offer that service to our customers not just because we might be able to offer a more informed opinion, but also as a matter of time management.

Consider this: with telecom, we're going to contact four providers. We're going to meet with each one to hear their "pitch." That's four hours. First, they're going to bring in their proposals. Four more hours. Second, they'll come back in for a Q & A. Four more hours. That's 12 hours. Third, I have to check references. That's four more hours. This does not count each provider calling me at least 15 times, asking for the business. That's at least 60 calls. Sometimes 100 calls. And next you have to make the decision. Then manage the changeover. It's complicated and technical. Finally, you start talking about the other provider contracts and start the process all over again.

We have found that just by managing these decisions, we have saved a company at least 40 hours. That's an entire week. They can spend that week making money.

Credibility.

This is a dog-eat-dog, very competitive, constantly changing business. The fact that we have navigated so much change for our customers gives us credibility. The clients we serve add credibility. We serve blue chip respected companies, as well as new successful companies. People select us when they value IT and understand its competitive advantage. They don't call us because we're the cheapest. You need to check the references thoroughly.

Come to the office.

You want an organization that invests in its own space. We encourage potential customers to drop by. They'll find people working here. They'll see people at the phones here. They'll see we've been here for awhile. They'll hear about our technicians in the field, reporting and traveling back to the office. They'll also see the dedicated engineers who are here, waiting for customers' calls. They'll see we are local and by looking at our equipment, they will confirm that we are a network operations center.

Locally staffed network operations center.

Our business is very easy to broker. Kind of like insurance. And in insurance, perhaps that's okay. Our business is more dynamic. Technology is not "one size fits all." But some technology companies try to do that. They broker everything out. You have to own it. There's no way to control quality if you don't.

Scheduled business review meeting.

In this meeting, one of our senior technology specialists visits your business to help you obtain and use the innovation you need. We help you understand what your options are and how technology can make you more money.

Another example. Maybe a year ago, you couldn't afford that scanner, but now it's so much cheaper, and you can afford two if you need them. The price of technology continues to drop, and we can keep you informed about new options. We show you technology that reduces customer transactions and makes doing business with you easier.

Data center ownership.

This is a center with racks and racks of computer equipment. It takes the place of you having to invest in new technology. You are using our state of the art equipment, at a fraction of the cost. Instead of hundreds of thousands of dollars, you're paying a couple of thousand dollars a month.

We have invested in our own data centers. We are not brokering. We want to control the quality and the speed. If someone is not investing in their own business, it should tell you something about their level of business. Data centers are expensive. They cost over half a million dollars. We have three at the time of this printing.

The provider is rock solid.

Take a look at their business. How long have they been in business? How long do their employees stick around? Is their business growing? Have they had to lay people off? Are they public or private? Do they have a board of advisers? How do they train? How do they seek to improve?

We Found the Win-Win!

I was at a large hospital recently and met with the senior officers. They are about to initiate a very large CRM, Customer Relationship Management program. This hospital is non-profit, and CRM is critical to their revenues through fundraising.

They did a CRM implementation ten years ago. Guess what happened when it was finished? The implementation vendors left, taking with them all the knowledge. The hospital also found out the contractors didn't understand some of their core values. And how could they? After all, they only had a few meetings.

As we were talking, the CEO pointed out that their IT people spend 80 percent of their time supporting the user. Tactical things. Keeping the lights on.

They were answering problems such as fixing a mouse, fixing a screen that won't come on. That left 25 percent of their time to work on strategic thinking. Working on the CRM project.

What's the best use of their time? Strategic, of course.

So, the solution was obvious. Let my company keep the light on while their IT got the CRM up and running. That way, they can design a CRM more effectively because they understand the values of the organization. Plus, they keep all the knowledge.

We create a win-win. We save them money and keep their staff focused on the strategic, not the tactical. To survive in this competitive environment, 80 percent of IT's time should be spent on strategic initiatives, and 20 percent or less should be spent on the tactical.

A pygmy is blindly following the old model instead of looking for ways to innovate.

> "So, here is the litmus test. If it's tactical, outsource it. If you have your in house people working on day to day tactical issues, odds are good the strategic (and most important) projects are suffering from lack of attention. They are on the back burner. How many times have we heard that a project is late because internal IT is just "too busy."

But so many CIOs get so caught up in the tactical that they

don't do any strategic. Here are some questions for you.

In the last six months, have you seen your IT Director...

- **Pull a cable?**

- **Swap out a mouse?**

- **Crawl around under a desk?**

- **Install a PC for someone?**

- **Install a server?**

- **Complain about working nights and weekends?**

If so, you may have the wrong model.

Here are some more questions you should ask:

- **When was the last time we experienced an outage?**

- **When was the last time we did a full test-restore of our backup?**

- **Do we have a disaster recovery plan? When was the last time we tested it?**

- **When was the last time our network got a physical? (Maybe it could be the same time the CEO goes for a physical)**

- **Do we know for a fact the state of our network?**

We help our customers know the answers to questions like these.

What Sets Us Apart?

From ten thousand feet, maybe it looks like we're all the same, but there are some big differences. I've already mentioned some.

Our in-depth engagement methodology also sets us apart. It's a primary, involved technical and financial network assessment we share with the stakeholders of the business.

There are three pieces to it:

First, the CEO baseline.

This is an executive summary of all things technological. We compare and contrast the organization with industry standards and best practices.

"It's in plain, easy to understand, non technical business language."

It's specific to the CEO's business and explains what's going on as it relates to all things technological.

Second, the CFO Technology Reconciliation.

This is a financial document detailing the total cost of ownership of all things technical, person and machine. It offers a side-by-side comparison with similar organizations. This document shows the total return on investment of technology. It also shows options for leveraging the technology to maximize business objectives.

Many businesses overspend on equipment. Why purchase top of the line equipment if you don't need it? There are all kinds of reasons. Many IT departments like bragging rights. This happens in data centers all over America, and the CEO has no clue. They'll buy a Ferrari when a golf cart would be fine.

Third, the CIO Technical Scorecard.

This is a highly detailed, technical document that addresses components connected to the network. They are scored against industry standard best practices. It also compares the number of people on staff with industry standards.

For example, industry standards say one person can handle 471 trouble tickets a month. So if you have ten people on your internal help desk and you're processing a thousand tickets a month, you've got eight people too many.

I'm not necessarily advocating firing those people, but if your list of projects is five pages deep, something's wrong with your allocation of IT personnel.

With these three forms of empirical data, we can compare your business to industry standards and benchmarks. Once you do that, you can start solving problems and reaching goals.

> **"You can use technology as a transformative tool to grow your business. IT can be a key differentiator between you and your competition."**

Executive Overview

We have a service in which we come in for a day and do a broad assessment. We tell an organization where there's a problem. We tell them the risk level. We call it an Executive Overview. At that point, they know if they're in good shape or bad shape. Some companies want us to go deeper, so we'll spend more than one day.

> **"It's a very small amount of money to prevent a problem that could cost huge amounts of money."**

We also have assessments that take considerably longer and are more in-depth. For those, we give a large report that provides documentation down to serial numbers, date of manufacture, connectivity map, and service agreements. It's basically a bible for the technical engineers. That way, it's not stored in one person's head.

All of the above cases are neutral evaluations. They are not sales pitches. Most companies are flying blind. They don't know when or where the next disaster is going to hit. This provides some insurance. Some peace of mind. We give you a plan to correct existing problems.

> **"A well-documented Network is a recoverable Network when disaster strikes."**

Selective Service

We also help in the hiring process. If a company is looking to hire an internal IT person, we can help interview and secure the best candidate. Often, we even conduct the interview so the CEO or CIO can observe. He can pay attention to the candidate's poise, people skills, knowledge, and experience.

Why Assess Your IT Department?

I have seen lemonade stands operate better than some IT departments. Why hasn't there been a change?

> **"Because the CEO doesn't know enough about IT to recognize it. He may know there's a problem, but he doesn't know how to fix it."**

The CEO can recognize when changes are needed in other areas. If the company started with a bookkeeper, when revenues became 50 or 100 times what they used to be, other financial positions were added, including a CFO.

Why?

Because the CEO knows that this is a position that has to evolve.

But he doesn't know that about IT. He assumes the IT department is good enough.

And the CIO may be good enough to keep the machines working. The problem is there's no vision. He's not building systems the company can use to a competitive advantage.

What does that mean?

Well, for one thing, it means you are leaving yourself wide open for all kinds of problems. For another thing, it means you may not even know about them until after they happen.

I was sitting in a conference room last week with the senior officers of a mid-size organization – a few hundred employees. One of their first comments was how happy they were that my team was getting involved. I asked why.

Because they had just learned the IT department had been reading the senior officers' emails. For a long time.

Guess what. Your emails are being read, too.

Internal IT people read email.

Why? They like to be in the know.

The IT director of one organization proudly announced what his Christmas bonus would be . . . two weeks before the Christmas bonuses were sent out. He had looked at an email from the accounting department and there was the bonus spreadsheet.

So, he was able to say, "Hey Fred, you're getting two hundred dollars less than Jean is."

"This is where a neutral, third party can help."

Let's face it. Everybody has strengths, and everybody has weaknesses. Everyone has different kinds of experience.

I use a large, multi-disciplined accounting firm in Tennessee.

Why do I use them instead of a two person accounting practice? As a matter of fact, we used to use a two person accounting firm. Then, something came up in which they weren't too strong. So I switched.

What I like about them is that if I need to talk about tax, we can talk about federal tax, state tax, or tax in another state. There is someone who has expertise and experience in this area.

If I want to talk about borrowing money and structuring debt, there is someone to provide expert advice and direction.

If I want to talk about charitable giving, wealth management, and tax credits regarding employees, they cover all of that.

So, what you look for in a third party is depth of experience as well as breadth of experience. You want a third party to come in with the ability to analyze. This is not one person, but a team.

In IT applications, you're looking for a third party that can analyze technical applications, physical infrastructure, operating satellite facilities, and so on. You want a team that can give you the right information at the right time.

In any organization, you have one person in IT who is the smartest of the IT lot. He's the tallest pygmy. But, he's only going to know what he knows. Especially if he's been in the organization for a long time. He's not going to be current on what's going on out there. Things change, and he certainly doesn't know what's going on in other organizations.

One of our strengths is we're inside hundreds of organizations. We can say,

"Hey, another company had that same kind of issue, and here's how they dealt with it."

So we take our cumulative base of knowledge and we help our customers. That helps us make strategic suggestions to help a company leverage their technology to increase profits and have a competitive advantage.

We show how the IT department should not just keep the lights on, but should also take the company to the next level through technology.

A neutral, third party doesn't have a dog in the hunt. We don't have an agenda. We are not trying to protect turf. We are not reading your email.

An internal employee is going to defend his mistakes, if he even knows they were mistakes. Maybe he is not aware that he was operating outside of best practices. Maybe he is unwilling or unable to create security measures to prevent privacy breaches.

That's a drag to revenue. It shows the company is not concentrating on innovation.

"If IT is not driving innovation, then you've got the wrong IT group."

As a third party consultant, I'm always going to put your business first. I'm not going to hide anything. My job is to give you an accurate picture of where things are.

You're not going to see an IT Director say,

"Well, we are really overstaffed now. We could get by with half the people we have."

Having no IT audit from an independent source is incredibly dangerous. It's like not having a financial audit or review.

When my firm is hired to analyze an organization's IT application, we report in simple, concrete terms. We explain what's not working, what needs to be done, and what the risk exposure is at this time.

For example, we say,

> **"Your servers – boom – here's what we found.**
> **Your switches – boom – here's what we found.**
> **Your workstations . . .**
> **Your firewalls . . ."**

We put it in black and white, step by step, and we explain what needs to be done and why.

The CEO is not interested in technical jargon. He doesn't know those words. He doesn't want to know those words. He just wants the business to maximize its potential.

We're talking about objective analysis that will help the CEO understand where things are, why things are where they are, and the best way to proceed. That's what a CEO needs to hear in every area of the business, especially the IT department.

Knowledge Deficiency = Disaster!

We've found a startling fact. The best products out there are not always represented by the best sales people. And some mediocre products are represented by fabulous sales people. That's where a trusted adviser comes in.

Here's a great example.

We were hired by an IT director. Although he knew enough to

get his system up and running, he didn't know enough to grow the system as the company grew.

With 50 employees, it ran like a champ. With 100 employees, it crawled on its knees. He thought it was a piece of equipment. He thought the SAN (storage area network – think of a cabinet full of disk drives) was overtaxed.

Think of going into McDonald's at 2:00 in the afternoon. You get your order quickly. But then go back at supper time. There are a lot of demands, and it takes longer to get your food. You have to wait.

That's called IO. Input and Output. The more input you have, the longer it takes.

So the IT director thought he just needed a new SAN to speed up the process. Not a bad guess. And the manufacturer helped lead him to that guess. Why? It wants more revenue.

It turns out it wasn't the hardware that was causing the bottleneck. It was the way the software was set up.

This brings me back to the original question. Why have we been successful? We care about our customers.

> **"We help our customers not only maintain their business, but also improve their business through technology."**

We provide a cost efficient way of leveraging a technology budget to do incredible things. We provide an accurate assessment to allow an organization to understand where it is and where it needs to be.

CHAPTER SIX
The Bottom Line

There is a difference between value and cost.

You can have good and fast, but it won't be cheap.

You can have fast and cheap, but it won't be good.

You can have good and cheap, but it won't be fast.

We provide a checklist (included in this chapter) for what to look for in an IT provider. You should use it.

Our company is set apart by our baseline assessments and our Executive Overviews.

That takes the CEO out of the dark. It provides concrete terms to explain what is working, what isn't working, what needs to be done, and what the risk exposure is.

Have you ever assessed your IT department? How?

Are you using a trunk slammer?

7 | Why Outsourcing Is For You

I was talking to a client of mine the other day. His company does about 500 million dollars a year in revenue, selling industrial chemicals to large retail organizations.

He was complaining about his IT department.

I asked him if he owned a trucking company to ship all of his merchandise.

> "Oh, no. We use common carriers. We have a purchasing agent who manages our freight via third party logistics. It's a little too complicated and expensive for us to handle on our own. Rates change; tariffs change. We just don't have the expertise."
>
> "Then why are you running an IT company?"
>
> "Oh, we're not running an IT company."
>
> "Well, let's see, you have 18 IT employees. You have an IT budget of about nine million dollars. I know a lot of IT companies that don't have 18 employees."

He thought about that for a second.

I asked him why he would outsource trucking but not IT.

"I guess I've never thought about it."

He was running a good business, but he was also funding an IT business. He was good at one and not so good at the other.

They don't clean their own floors. They don't provide their own security. But they do their own IT. He has no idea what he's missing by having an IT department that's not contributing to the bottom line.

The key is to determine how to use technology. It is also to determine when you need to outsource a particular job. You probably already outsource at least certain parts of your accounting, your legal, your maintenance, your janitorial, your lawn and landscaping, and a few other things. It's not your core competency.

"In the same way, you should ask yourself whether IT is your core competency?"

It's hard to keep up. It's hard to know what's coming around the corner. So, the question is, should you be focusing on your business or funding an internal IT department?

That's not best practices. It's also not smart, any way you look at it. You lose speed to market of your products and services.

"You are spending a lot of money for an average service."

Or you could outsource it to an organization whose core competency is IT. This organization not only provides professional maintenance of your equipment and applications, but, more importantly, also provides you with knowledgeable, current advice on how technology can gain and keep customers.

It keeps you competitive.

Here's another advantage for outsourcing technology to companies like mine. We help you look down the road. We help you see emerging trends and preferences, and we show you how technology can meet those needs. We also are able to share marketing practices used by organizations in different industries.

We recommend a strategic marketing session where we talk about how technology can make your business grow and take it to the next level.

As I've shared in other parts of the book, outsourcing is the ultimate solution for almost every company, especially mid-size companies. Picture this:

- **You have state of the art computers on every desk. They're replaced with new ones every three years.**

- **You've outsourced your server, meaning you no longer have to maintain, upgrade, protect, or fix it.**

- **You never have any down time! Think of what that does for your business! You never lose data.**

- **Instead of a small staff of IT people, you now have a large team of up-to-date, certified, knowledgeable, strategic professionals.**

- **Your employees have 24/7 access to a technical support center that is extremely familiar with your company.**

- **When you're in Europe and need help with a download to your phone, you have the peace of mind to know that a capable person will be able to help you.**

Ready for the kicker? Often it's cheaper than what you're paying now!

We've Always Done it This Way

One definition of insanity is expecting a different result when you continue to repeat the same action.

I have had clients who have spent their money the same way only to discover they were getting the same results. It's like a sausage maker. You get out what you put in.

That's how you ultimately leverage technology. You have to realize that a change needs to take place. You don't have to spend more money. Just use it differently.

For example, more and more companies are saying,

"We don't want to spend our money to own servers."

Like it or not, that's where things are going. Because owning the server is just tip of the iceberg. There's the care and feeding of it. There are daily, weekly, and monthly procedures that need to be completed.

I call it weeding the garden.

Planting the garden is one thing. That's buying the server. But every day, there's some kind of weed – an antivirus, spam, the upkeep. You have to patch, you have to do things every day to keep the hackers out. You have to make sure you get a good backup. You have to test it. It's a daily process. The initial price is probably a tenth of the total cost.

So, companies are changing. They are deciding that if they use someone else's server, their capital expenditures can be diverted.

It helps with cyclical business. You can use more during peak times without paying for it for the rest of the year, and without having to weed the garden.

"The truth of the matter is the IT part of a business is in every part of the business. This is
true for a company that is ten people or 1,000
people. And the question quickly arises: Do
you want to be in the IT business or in the
business you started?"

Think about it. No department knows your company better
than the IT department.

Production knows production.

Warehouse knows warehouse.

But IT is in every department.

The director of IT should have a global understanding of IT's
footprint within each step of the company.

**"I want to see how we can reduce three days
off shipping."**

**"I want to see how we can ship three hours
after the order instead of three days."**

So why outsource? Ever hear the term, "This isn't your father's Chevrolet"? This isn't your father's operating environment
for business, either. A big part of the new environment has to do
with outsourcing.

Three Main Reasons to Outsource

1. Speed to market.

Let's look at the importance of Speed. If a customer needs
you, they don't want to get your voicemail. They want to talk to

you now or want you to call them back quickly.

They also don't want to have to wait on mail or even a fax.

Business has become instant. And if you can't serve your customers instantly, they'll find somebody who can. You can't serve your customers instantly with 5-year-old equipment. You've been holding onto it because you don't want to pay for new stuff, and you don't want to have lost time on the learning curve. Outsourcing saves you the capital expenditures and the lost time pain.

We talked about the new age we live in. There are competitors of yours who have seldom read a printed newspaper. They read it online. They just might take all your customers because they know how to get things done faster than you.

And if they're not competitors, they're customers. You have to understand them and cater to their buying practices.

We have all gotten the elephant customer, the one that we have been going after for months or years, and they finally say, "We want to do business with you."

Then all of a sudden we figure out, "Oops!" Why? Because the way we have to interact with them is electronically, and we are not ready for that. So what do you do? You can build it, but you really do not have the staff to do it.

Or you can outsource.

You have an opportunity, but you have to act on it fast. An internal staff cannot even touch it. Why? Probably because there are some pygmies there, but maybe not.

Maybe you have a good group, but this takes it to a different level of expertise that they do not have. Maybe they have been there too long.

2. Capital preservation.

I loved 2007 and early 2008 when the bankers kept calling on us saying, "Okay we want to give you this and here is a better deal." Capital was like gold coins on the street.

That is no longer the case. Outsourcing allows you to get that production and the processing. It allows you to achieve what you need but preserve capital. So instead of having a capital expenditure of $500,000, maybe you operationalize the expense and write a check for $15,000 a month – a whole lot easier to deal with.

How do you save money?

How do you spend your money wisely?

"Technology helps reduce manpower."

It eliminates timely chores. For example, while some medical centers do it the old fashioned way, my doctor has patients fill out the medical forms online before they come in. Among other things, it saves an office person from having to retype everything a patient wrote.

If a doctor sees 30 patients a day and you have ten doctors in a group, that's 300 patients a day. That's over 1,000 patients a week. See how technology saves money?

And instead of sending you a letter or making a phone call to remind you of your next office visit, the savvy doctor or dentist group is going to plug that in when you make the appointment. Then you are reminded by text and email, with no expense.

3. Your core competency.

I was with a client Friday, and we had that conversation. He is in the asphalt paving business, and he did not want to have an internal IT department.

They'd had it for years and years, and as the economy started having problems, they said,

> **"We do not do this well; we certainly don't know enough about it to wring all of the cost out of it."**

So they outsourced that to us and saved significant dollars. They were able to accelerate a timeline.

For him, getting out of the IT business meant he wasn't going to have to deal with IT staff turnover every 24 months.

He was able to preserve capital.

He was able to get a best of breed, state of the art system and eliminate his worries over downtime from here on out.

Technology Keeps Customers!

You also save and generate money in all kinds of ways by using technology. Let me give you an example. I buy my clothes from a well respected men's store here in Memphis. I've been a loyal customer for years.

I recently purchased three pairs of pants. I've been waiting on them for a month. My salesman tells me they are on backorder. That's simply not acceptable.

Technology could prevent the inventory from getting this low. It could allow my salesperson to know my preferences, my size and contact me regularly regarding what's new.

I like nice clothes. I am a regular customer. I am thinking about changing where I do business. If I am thinking about this, I guarantee you others are, too. If this company had outsourced their IT (instead of using the trunk slammer they use) to a reputable IT organization, how many customers would they keep and attract?

An unhappy customer talks, me being a case in point.

A happy customer also talks.

Is my clothes store taking a look at who buys clothes there and how they like to buy clothes?

The answer is no.

On the other hand, what if they had emailed me when the specific brands that I liked arrived?

Technology makes and can help keep customers!

Businesses have to think down the road. That's where your IT department needs to be helping you.

Is your CIO helping you with strategic decisions?

Here's a secret: once you take a new piece of equipment out of the box, if you return it, the manufacturer cannot sell it as new, even though it's never been used.

When the manufacturer gets it back, it's called an "open box return." The manufacturer is required to put it through the entire refurbishing process. So they sell it for about half of what a brand new machine costs. It has full warranty.

IT departments could save their companies thousands by buying these open box return items.

But IT people seldom go that route. They lack the knowledge and experience of a third party like me.

> **"So the question is, does your IT department work side by side with the other departments, to be an agent of change? Or is it mired in tactical quicksand and clueless about the future?"**

Either way, it pays to retain a company like ours to help you see purchasing options on top of the strategic options.

The more you outsource, the more you increase your competitive advantage.

CHAPTER SEVEN

The Bottom Line

If you outsource everything else in the world, why not outsource your IT?

As we've talked about, senior officers are often so busy working in the business, they don't work on the business. What does that mean?

- They should be able to ask questions about attracting and maintaining customers.

- They should be able to maximize the customer experience.

- They should be able to add services.

- They should be able to predict future trends.

- They should be able to know what technology you need to accomplish these goals. An outsourced organization like ours helps you get there.

Closing

D o you have a trusted IT adviser? If not, why not?

I hope you found this book valuable. In closing, I have one last piece of important advice.

Most successful CEOs surround themselves with trusted advisers with highly specialized knowledge and expertise – a CPA, an investment adviser, a lawyer, perhaps even an executive coach.

So, why don't you have someone you trust to advise you on IT strategy?

Technology – the data it provides and the productivity it enhances – is critical to the growth of your company. Year after year your firm spends large sums of money on IT. But do you know what you're getting? Do you know if the budget dollars are being wisely spent? Chances are, they are not.

Technological advances will continue to move faster and faster. So will the pace of business. Without a trusted adviser, you may move rapidly in the wrong direction, causing you to lose market share and competitive advantage.

You need someone outside the company – a trusted adviser you can count on to give you the straight up facts. No politics, no empire building. Just a solid strategy that will positively leverage technology to transform your firm and position it for the future.

As a CEO myself, I face many of the same business issues as you do. Feel free to call on me at anytime, regardless of where you are located. I'd be happy to point you in the right direction to find a reliable, trusted adviser.

Please drop me an email at mark@sacorp.net. Again, don't hesitate to get in touch if I can be of further assistance.

Regards,

Mark Giannini
CEO, Service Assurance

Value Add

Value Add 1 | Cloud Computing

We have past, present, and the future.

The past is the land where time stood still.

The present is where we are now. Organizations are doing more and more leveraging of technology and outsourcing.

The future is cloud computing. Customers will no longer own their own servers. They're using someone else's. Many experts are predicting that in a very short period of time, at least 25 percent of organizations will own no IT assets. They outsource it all. It's moving fast.

It would be moving even faster if the CEO understood it. You know who doesn't want him to understand it? The IT department. At least the pygmy in the IT department.

"The pygmy is not interested in the company's benefit. He's interested in his future. And outsourcing could be career threatening to a pygmy."

There are local servers. These are called private clouds. For example, one of our clients wants to move everything from their Data Center over to ours.

The reason they want to do this is very simple. Two months ago, someone a couple of floors above them got upset and stopped up all the toilets. They did this on the weekend.

On Monday, my client found water all over the floor of their data center. So, they want to get the data center out of that building. They want the peace of mind that this won't happen again.

Value Add 2 | IT Termination

The other day, I got a call from a CEO. As they grew, the company went from a three-person IT department to a completely outsourced one. Ten years ago, an IT Director did not work out. We helped pick up the slack, and the company continued to function perfectly.

A second person on their IT staff left and, again, they didn't miss a beat. The CEO called me over the weekend and said,

> **"We've got a problem. One of our senior level executives has violated our code of trust so we are not going to keep him around anymore. I'm going to need someone here at a certain time to disable his network access while I'm having the termination talk with him."**

We created an IT Termination Checklist you need for any employee to protect yourself from any shenanigans and havoc on the network. Remember, in less than five seconds they can destroy anything if they know what they're doing. Some, if they've got a friend who is good and malicious, can simply plug a thumb drive in that will auto boot, auto execute, and create havoc.

As we continued to talk, the CEO said,

"I love our arrangement because I can call you and have a business conversation, and there's no emotion. Before you came along, I couldn't have had this conversation days in advance with an internal person, just because of office politics and the grapevine.

She liked to gossip, and she would have told somebody and sworn them to secrecy. Of course, they would have done the same thing, and before you know it, 20 people know and the person who is going to be terminated suddenly knows, and if he does want to do some bad things, he can.

One of the other things is that when I talk to you, I feel I'm having a business discussion. We're not talking about emotion, and we're not talking about IT because quite candidly, rarely do I ever talk about IT."

What we were talking about was function. We want to protect the corporate data assets, and he's asking me to make sure that gets done.

He didn't ask me what computer this person had. He didn't ask me where this data lived. He didn't ask me about gigs or panel size, because it didn't matter.

He was right. This is about business; it's not about technology. Technology is the vehicle the business runs on.

Then he said,

> **"I grew up in the age of "Green Acres," with
> the old switchboard phone system in the town.
> Sarah, the operator, would plug a cord in and
> connect you to your other party. But, of course,
> Sarah always listened in.**
>
> **I could never send an email about anything
> like this because the IT department would read
> it."**

There's always that grapevine. You've got it at your office; I've got it at mine, and there's always little rumblings of who's doing what. Who got in trouble over the weekend, who's having marital problems at home, who got a new boat ... whatever it may be. What you often find is IT is the center of the grapevine.

It reminds me of a senior engineer who bought a brand new Volkswagen Beetle. He put one bumper sticker on it: I read your email.

The CEO continued,

> **"Now since we've outsourced everything to
> you, when we send you an email, we don't worry
> about it. You don't care about our politics. All
> you care about is keeping our business going."**

That's like when I take my car to the mechanic. The mechanic doesn't care when he notices that I'm reading a James Patterson book as opposed to "War and Peace." He's concerned about fixing the car.

You can get some real peace of mind that an outsourced professional organization is not interested in your emails. They're interested in supporting, maintaining, and/or fixing the network.

If you've got an IT Director that might be concerned about what Mary Lou's doing because he and Mary Lou went out for a drink and he thinks there may be some romance there. I guarantee you he's reading every one of Mary Lou's emails, and that's taking away from what he should be doing.

But it's also violating all sorts of privacy issues and can create all kinds of problems if something happens and suddenly you need to get rid of Mary Lou.

Your IT department is looking at not only every email you send, but they could very easily be archiving every email you send and you wouldn't know it –and they're looking at every website so they know what you're doing, and how you're doing it.

The CEO would have never gone to his IT people and told them this person was going to be terminated next Thursday, because that person would have known 24 hours after the CEO told them.

But to us, it's just a business process. We don't care that this person is being fired. It's not our business. We are there to do a task: to fix a problem and deliver a result.

How to Fire An Employee

Firing an employee is never easy.

In the old days, while it was difficult, it was relatively easy to protect yourself. You would bring them into your office, shut the door, have a conversation, maybe with HR there. You would escort them to their desk to gather their belongings, and that would be that. Nobody likes to fire anyone, but it's unfortunately a necessary part of the job; it's what we signed up for.

But in this day in age, it's a little bit different. Actually it's a lot different, and some companies do not really know the proper way to terminate an employee and protect themselves from an IT standpoint.

You need a Termination Checklist.

If you have ever been on the receiving end of a disgruntled employee and a Termination Checklist wasn't followed, you know that employee can wreak havoc that can cost hundreds of thousands of dollars. If there is not a good backup and disaster recovery plan place, he could create loss of data forever.

I received a phone call from a client this week. He was in a panic.

The CFO said,

"Mark, I need to talk. I've got a problem. We've got an employee that we are going to have to let go next week, and, quite candidly, I don't trust 'Bob' to tell him. I'm afraid of what might happen because this person has a key position, and we don't want them to do anything harmful to our data."

He went on to say that if this employee deleted what's on his workstation, they'd never get it back. This is a company that does a lot of marketing, so who knows what damage could be done by simply erasing data. But the red flag is they did not trust their internal person to do the firing.

So, why can't Bob do it? Well he could, but he's friends with this person, and their families hang out together so he's scared to tell that person. It's a classic example of the distrust in IT management.

The CFO, of course, is protecting the company's interests when a key employee is going to be terminated. So we were able to take images of his PC so no matter what he did, the company was protected. Even if this person, say, threw his PC out the window, it wouldn't be a problem because we can recover everything.

But the underlying point of the story is management and IT don't sit on the same side of the table in many cases. And as this company continues to grow and they continue to experience IT problems, we envision them being able to understand that IT, while it's important, it's a tactical function.

Email and protecting yourself – it's tactical. What's on that computer is strategic. So this company will bring in a strategic person to create the work, but they look for an outsourced arrangement to protect the work and to keep it running.

If you don't have an IT Termination Checklist, you need one. You'll find ours on the next page.

IT Termination Checklist

- Disable user and change his/her password. Do not delete the account yet – you may need it for something unforeseen.

- Check all server services to make sure the user did not configure a server with his/her account.

- Have all administrators change their passwords immediately.

- Change the passwords on all local administrator accounts of servers that are not domain controllers.

- Possibly change the password on all local administrator accounts on all workstations.

- Check all server services. If one is set to use the administrator account, change the password.

- Check to make sure no users are in administrative groups who do not belong there.

- Have everyone with remote access change their passwords immediately or revoke their access.

- Have all users change their passwords.

- Check all remote access systems for back doors or hidden accounts.

- Change any wireless encryption keys.

Value Add 3 | Demystifying the Data Center

Most CEOs can do everything in their business except IT. But if a CEO could understand how a data center works, he would learn it's really not that complicated. There's a server (think of it as a big PC with lots of memory), a CPU (think of it as the engine), and some disk drives (for storage). There's a power supply or two. There's a network card (that's how you attach to your PC). There are switches. And there's a video output to the monitor.

That's a simplified version of your data center. When you break it down, there aren't that many pieces. And all the pieces are easily understandable. Once you look under the hood, you understand. And it doesn't have to take that long.

What is a computer?

A computer is an electronic device that executes the instructions in a program. A computer has four functions:

- **Input – accepts data**

- **Processing – processes data**

- **Output – produces data**

- **Storage – stores results**

Some basic terms

- Hardware – the physical parts of the computer
- Software – the programs (instructions) that tell the computer what to do
- Data – individual facts (first name, price, quantity ordered)
- Information – data that has been put into a useful form (a complete mailing address)

What makes a computer powerful?

- Speed – a computer can perform billions of actions per second
- Reliability – failures are usually due to human error, one way or another
- Storage – a computer can store huge amounts of data

Personal systems

Computers for personal use come in all shapes and sizes, from tiny PDAs (personal digital assistants) to desktop computers.

When talking about PCs, most people probably think of the standard desktop computer.

But the market for smaller PCs is expanding rapidly. Software is becoming available for Netbooks, PDAs, and Smartphones.

With a Tablet PC, you use an electronic stylus to write on the screen. It saves your work just like you wrote it (as a picture), or you can let the Hand Recognition (HR) software turn your chicken-scratch into regular text.

Server

The term "server" actually refers to a computer's function rather than to a specific kind of computer. A server runs a network of computers. It handles the sharing of equipment like printers and the communication between computers on the network. For such tasks, a computer would need to be somewhat more capable than a desktop computer. It would need:

- **More power**

- **Larger memory**

- **Larger storage capacity**

- **High-speed communications**

What is input?

Everything we tell the computer is input.

Types of input are:

- **Data – the raw facts given to the computer.**

- **Programs – the sets of instructions that direct the computer.**

- **Commands – special codes or key words the user inputs to perform a task. These can be selected from a menu of commands like "Open" on the File menu. They may also be chosen by clicking on a command button.**

- **User response – the user's answer to the computer's question, such as choosing OK, YES, or NO or by typing in text, for example, the name of a file.**

What is output?

Output is data that has been processed into useful form, now called "information."

Types of output are:

- **Hard copy – printed on paper or stored on other permanent media**

- **Soft copy – displayed on a screen or stored by other non-permanent means**

Categories of output:

- **Text documents – reports, letters, etc.**

- **Graphics – charts, graphs, pictures, etc.**

- **Multimedia – combination of text, graphics, video, and audio**

What is storage?

Storage refers to the media and methods used to keep information available for later use. Some things will be needed right away, others won't be needed for extended periods of time. So different methods are appropriate for different uses.

Remember from early times all the kinds of things stored in Main Memory.

"Primary Storage is Main Memory."

Main Memory consists of the operating system, applications, input/output system, working storage, and usused storage.

It keeps track of what is currently being processed.

It's volatile (power off erases all data).

For Main Memory, computers use RAM, or Random Access

Memory. This uses memory chips and is the fastest and most expensive type of storage.

"Secondary Storage is called Auxiliary Storage."

This is what is not currently being processed. This is the stuff filed away, but ready to be pulled out when needed.

It is nonvolatile (power off does not erase).

Auxiliary Storage is used for:

- **Input – data and programs**

- **Output – saving results of processing**

So, Auxiliary Storage is where you put last year's tax info, addresses for old customers, programs you may or may not ever use, data you entered yesterday – everything not being used right now.

The types of Auxiliary Storage used most often involve some type of magnetic disk. These come in various sizes and materials. This method uses magnetism to store the data on a magnetic surface. Advantages include:

- **High storage capacity**

- **Reliability**

- **Direct access to data**

A drive spins the disk quickly underneath a read/write head, which does what its name says. It reads data from a disk and writes data to a disk.

A common type of magnetic disks is the hard disk. These consist of one or more metal platters sealed inside a case. The hard disk is usually installed inside the computer's case, though there are removable and cartridge types, also.

Technically, the hard drive controls the motion of the hard disks, which contain the data. But most people use "hard disk" and "hard drive" interchangeably.

An entirely different method of recording data is used for optical disks.

You may guess from the word "optical" that it has to do with light. You'd be exactly right!

Optical disks contain peaks and valleys in a plastic layer on a circular disk read by a laser.

Value Add 4 | Types of Pygmies

The Lifer
I walked into an organization yesterday, and I could tell everyone was tense.

The reason? Everyone's computer was down. No email, no Internet, no outside connectivity. They couldn't do anything on the computer except play games.

It was the third working day with systems being down and preventing them from doing significant work.

The IT director decided to do an upgrade on Saturday, and it didn't work. And he failed to make a backup.

The problem for this somewhat small business – less than one hundred employees – was the IT director didn't know what he was doing.

But he had been there a long time.

What now?

Well, either he gets serious about his job and gets some serious training or . . . he leaves.

Now this person is not unpopular. As a matter of fact, no one wants him to leave. They just want things to get better immediately. It's kind of like having a popular football coach. He's friendly. He's popular. The only thing wrong is he hasn't won a game in three seasons.

He's not leaving. He's trying the same things and getting the same results. And he's making a mess.

One of the managers said,

"Well, I guess these things just happen."

That's a very generous manager. These things don't have to happen! You don't have to settle for that style of support.

Empire Builder

You've got a CEO who's trying to double the business every year. That means a lot of growth, which often leads to some confusion. And you've got an IT director who is quickly getting in over his head.

He's trying to build the IT department – to keep up – and doesn't know what to do.

But this IT director is going to create his own empire within the organization. He has power. He wants to establish as many walls as he can to fortify his empire, which makes it harder for you to get rid of him.

Then there's the Business Within a Business Empire Builder. He takes it a step further. He runs his own business within yours. Maybe he's using your IT department to do service for other organizations. He's stealing. He's using the company's resources for personal gain.

A few weeks ago, we did a network assessment (something I highly recommend) for an organization. When I shared the results with the CEO, I asked,

> **"Do you own a company called ABC?"**
> **"No. Why?"**
> **"What about the DEF Company?"**
> **"No. Why?"**
> **"Well, we found them running on your server and your data center."**
> **"What does that mean?"**
> **"They are using your resources to run their websites, their emails, their file servers, and their line of business applications."**

We have also discovered IT departments that order laptops never used by the IT department. They were used by sons and daughters of IT department employees. We also found one purchased for an employee's girlfriend.

Mr. No Accountability

How would you like to come in for your job evaluation and have your supervisor say,

> **"Bob, to be honest, I don't have a clue what you do, so why don't you just tell me how things are going?"**

You give a glowing account of your work ethic, your contributions, and hint that you got here just in time to save the company.

Your supervisor then pats you on the back and says, "Keep up the good work!"

You didn't tell him about the developmental issues you need to work on.

You didn't tell him about mistakes you made.

You didn't tell him anything bad about your work.

Welcome to the world of IT accountability.

The CEO thinks the IT department is doing a good job and has met expectations if they stay within their budget. The CEO thinks the IT department is doing a good job if emails can be read and computers are running. Pretty much, beyond that, the CEO doesn't know what to expect. So he just doesn't ask critical questions.

Hmm. Is that how job performance evaluations are conducted in other departments? HR? Safety? Facilities? Accounting? Sales?

What happens to an employee with no accountability? Unless he's a descendent of Abraham Lincoln or George Washington, he's probably not going to get better.

That's putting it mildly.

He's going to get lazy.

I was at a client's business today. We were discussing an assessment he wanted us to perform. In other words, a performance review. I listened to the CEO say,

"I think everything is perfect. We are in compliance. We never go down. I don't know much about IT but all seems great. I just want it confirmed."

The CEO didn't come into town on a turnip truck last week. He knew sometimes things aren't always as they seem. But sometimes they are. I assured him we would let him know our results. He said, "I'd love to show my board an independent assessment confirmed we have an outstanding IT department."

He also realized he had 12 locations and depended heavily on IT. What if there was more they could be doing? What if they weren't up on some of the latest cloud computing options? What if they missed a strategic opportunity to help make the company more competitive?

I found out the IT director had a young family and was very family minded. Do you think he went home, said "Hello" to his kids and dove straight into industry journals and trade journals?

Absolutely not. He's going to spend time throwing the ball and watching a movie. They're going to have family nights and school nights and homework and baths and bedtime stories.

I love that. But one person can never keep his company current on IT strategies. There just aren't enough hours in the day.

What's wrong with a CIO who is a family man? Absolutely nothing! But the fact remains, every day he's getting further and further behind.

The Wolf Pack

They move from company to company as a team. You have one leader and a bunch of "yes" people. They know how to cover each other's backsides. They look good and usually talk well. They want to write business cases. They actually do very little compared to what they could do.

When the leader gets the next position, you see him take several folks from your IT department with him.

Here are a couple of more reasons why the Wolf Pack is not good.

One, everyone is following the leader just like they followed the leader at the previous company where the entire team worked. So there are not really any new, fresh, innovative ideas, and there is not what I would call creative or constructive dissension. When the leader presents an idea, the team just blindly goes along as they always have done.

Two, they have implemented similar solutions in the past at their previous employer, and while that solution may have worked there, it does not necessarily translate well to the new company. But they always seem to default to whatever it was they did before.

Mr. We've Always Done It This Way

They are so closed-minded, they don't even see innovation happen. They only figure it out, if they do, when the business closes. This strategy works sometimes, like if you're making homemade ice cream, but not in IT issues. Things do not stay the same. Customer demographics change. Customer preferences change. Ordering preferences change. Shipping, marketing and communication options change. The IT department that can't lead the way is the department that may drag the organization out of business.

The Plumber

You walk through your building and see the CIO running cables and changing out equipment. It's nice to know he doesn't mind hands-on work, but is this really the best use of his time? Right now he's doing everything tactical and nothing strategic. Is he there to work on the "plumbing" or to work with you strategically to determine how technology can help your customers?

He is focusing on the operational problems. And he doesn't realize what vision is about.

Hyper Lawn Mower

I've heard it said by more than one corporate officer that the IT department seems to make up work. It's a method of job security. "It's like they mow the lawn five times a week," one CEO told me.

"They seem busy, but nothing's getting done."

They are not accomplishing anything, but they stay and look busy. They are doing work, but not making any progress. They are not helping the company stay competitive.

I've heard this from the CEOs of billion-dollar companies. "They're like my five year old at supper," one senior officer said. "He pushes the food he doesn't want to eat all over the plate, but never gets around to actually eating it."

The IT department throws up barriers like, "Before we do this, let's do a Proof of Concept."

So they look at 90 different scenarios.

My comment is always, "Why?"

The IT's reply is always, "We just need to see what we can do."

I point out that out of those 90 scenarios only ten fit the budget, so why look at them?

It reminds me of five people on the 40th floor of a building, learning that there's a small fire on the 20th floor. One person probably is too scared or intimidated to offer any suggestion. Two people want to look at all the options for escape, including helicopters and rescues from superheroes. Meanwhile the

135

other two people have called security, found an escape route, and are helping the others get to safety.

Not only does it not make any sense for an IT department to look at every scenario, but it also costs valuable time, months in many cases. There is also the frustration of management seeing nothing is going on. That is assuming and maintaining the role of the tallest pygmy.

"Activity is not Productivity!"

The Cat Burglar

Sometimes the CIO is a fraud. He doesn't know nearly as much as he's given credit for. So he tries to keep the CEO in the dark on what he does know and what the IT department is doing. He doesn't want an audit. He doesn't want scrutiny. He realizes he's the tallest pygmy and just doesn't want to be found out.

Circus Trainer

This IT director is big on protocol and procedures. He loves steps and forms. He reminds me of the trainer in the big cage with the lions and tigers. What does he have them doing? Jumping through as many hoops as possible.

Characteristics of a Pygmy

Goes about business as usual   Just keeps the lights on

Expensive   Constantly saying "no"

Closed-minded   Afraid of change

Makes excuses   Disappointing

Tactical rather than strategic   Building an empire

Hidden from the outside   Part of the problem

Hates being measured   Runs away from problems

Talks about maintenance costs   Wants to complicate things

Procrastinator   Resistent to new ideas

You might have a pygmy if . . .

- IT projects are late

- You find yourself avoiding the IT department as much as possible

- Your IT department comes in over budget frequently

- Your system crashes regularly or you're without email services often

- You can't understand what your CIO says

- The IT department is not service oriented

- The IT department is not making you money

- You can't get a report without going through the IT department

Characteristics of a Good IT Department

Innovative	Productive
Transformative	Makes a good ROI
Your partner	Focused on the bottom line
Agent of change	Open to ideas
Decisive	Looks the CEO in the eye
On time and budget	Executes well
Strategic	Collaborative
"Can do" attitude	Visible
Part of the solution	Loves service levels
Can talk competitive advantage	Wants to simplify
Helps retain customers	Adaptive
Produces results	A go-to person

Embraces and addresses compliance and governance

You have a strong IT department if . . .

- You never experience any down time

- IT is always looking for ways to drive revenue and improve the customer experience

- IT looks for ways to differentiate you from your competitors

- Users are happy and productive

- Your CIO is looking outside of IT for ways to improve the business

- Projects are executed on time and on budget

Value Add 5 | Why People Come to Me

The only reason people want to talk to my company is that they're in pain:

- **Their guy just left.**

- **They are in serious financial or competitive trouble (the two go hand in hand) and they don't know what to do about it.**

- **They just had a major IT mishap. Maybe through fire, heat, or water damage. Maybe through lost information. Maybe through damaged backup.**

The CEO finally couldn't take it anymore. Nothing worked right. Email was often not working. It took forever to download a file. It took IT days to comply with a request.

A college came to me with some legitimate concerns about their IT costs. They said they didn't have enough money to do what they really had to do with IT.

It turned out their IT guys just didn't have enough knowledge. We were able to replace and maintain their IT equipment cheaper than they were doing it now, using their old stuff.

Let's face it. IT guys aren't a favorite of bosses anyway.

Many IT guys (not all) have poor people skills. They are like little dogs, nipping at the boss's heels, saying, "I need money."

Often the IT guy doesn't have the skill set to understand or say to the CEO, "Here are your goals, and here's what you need."

And even the IT guys who are loved are often burned out, overworked, and need help. (And don't forget, loved guys sometimes leave!)

We are here to help their organization do great work. In essence, our presence allows them to do higher level work.

If this were a hotel, we would be the ones to help free "Bob" up. If we find him cleaning the toilets and the rooms, we take that job and allow him to work on more strategic and pressing items.

At the same time, we are able to save a company significant money through outsourcing. A company – the hotel – outsources everything to us. They use our server, they lease brand new equipment from us, and they utilize not just Bob, but an entire team of experienced, knowledgeable, certified staff members. And here's the best part. Often it is not only an incredible jump in quality and service, but also significantly cheaper!

That's Not My Job

Have you ever participated in a trade show? Have you ever tried to run an extension cord to your booth at the trade show? You were told, "Oh no, you can't do that. We'll have to get the electrical union down here." Any time you wanted to do anything, you had to find the union with that particular function.

Many IT departments are very similar. They have their own silos. One silo can only work on IP addresses. Another works on user names. Another works on resetting passwords. To get anything done, you have to go through five of these silos.

It slows work down tremendously. It causes your employees to avoid the IT department as much as possible. It makes you less efficient in many ways.

Value Add 6 | Modern Industrialization's Last Frontier – IT

Business executives see IT infrastructure like they viewed manufacturing 20 years ago – an opportunity to apply new concepts to an expensive part of their firm, turning a burden into a strategic asset.

This leads to modern IT expectations:

- **Enabling strategic business expansions**

- **Expediting new product rollouts**

- **Rapidly integrating acquisitions**

- **Using technology to outperform the competition**

- **Achieving high performance business outcomes**

How are costs reduced?

- Talent Management (labor arbitrage) – the right skill set, when you need it, only for as long as you need it
- High Performance processes and tools to measure and track expectations and results
- Consolidated call center to manage technical resources, improve service level, and reduce cost
- Advanced offsite and onsite service and project management delivered from the same delivery model
- IT infrastructure rationalization – Internal IT employees are the most expensive and often most inefficient way to support IT
- Leverage of scale – Support ratios (staff to PC's) range from 1:125 to 1:600

Path to IT infrastructure delivery optimization

- Determine IT's role in the corporate strategy/vision
- Assessment of existing IT infrastructure and assets, relationship of IT assets and business strategy, areas of internal competence, and areas in need of improvement
- Ascertain speed of change and Service Assurance's role
- Design an optimized service delivery model specific to the client
- Create and implement improvement processes
- Monitor, manage, and reinforce a culture of service

Value Add 7 | What Makes a Successful CIO?

O ne man's opinion:

First

They should have a multifaceted background in operations, accounting, and IT.

Second

They should approach their world from an operations perspective first (i.e., what is it we need without any regard for accounting or IT?), then from an accounting perspective (i.e., what are the accounting and internal control requirements related to the envisioned solution?), next from an IT perspective last (i.e., what technology challenges would we face with the envisioned solution?).

This is obviously a generalization, since sometimes it's important to understand the technology-enabling possibilities before a solution is recommended (i.e., if you don't know teleportation exists, you will forever be working on how to improve the airline industry).

Third

They should think from a business perspective at all times. "Why" to do something is even more important than "what" should be done. Focusing on high-enterprise value IT is eons better than IT managed by help desk. There will always be opportunity costs. Picking the initiatives that are the most strategically aligned with the business is better than taking the IT purist view of having the best technology or spending the least amount on IT.

There are also some important competencies that go along with these basic tenants.

Good communication skills (and even better listening skills) are mandatory. The key with this competency is the ability to tell good stories that captivate your audience. Written and oral wizardry is a must. The ability to frame stories your audience can relate to is equally important.

Mentoring/coaching is also paramount for success. You can't do it all alone. A good team to support the vision is key.

Pragmatic decision making trumps perfection. Making every decision as if you are spending your own money leads to better decision making.

Larry Shutzberg
Vice President & CIO
Evergreen Packaging

About the Author

Mark Giannini's 23-plus years of experience in the Information Technology field include time at IBM, EMC, and 20 years as the founder and CEO of Service Assurance, the largest regional Technology Support and Managed Services provider in the Mid-South. Service Assurance is a leader in working with organizations to streamline IT operations and leverage the capital investment of the enterprise in IT infrastructure and support. Service Assurance also has the largest U.S. Staffed Help Desk in the Mid-South, operating 7x24x365.

Mark is a graduate of Christian Brothers University in Memphis, Tenn., with a B.S. in Marketing and a concentration in Information Technology Management. He is very active in the community, serving on several boards as a director, including The Dixon Gallery and Gardens, Boys and Girls Club of Greater Memphis, Visible Music College, Beale Street Caravan, Memphis Botanic Gardens, The Leadership Academy, Christian Brothers University, and the Greater Memphis Chamber. Mark has spoken nationally on such topics as Disaster Recovery, Business Continuity Planning, and Using Information Technology as a Competitive Weapon.

Mark serves as a senior adviser to many CEOs of privately held businesses in Memphis and the Mid-South.

Contact Mark Giannini

Need help with your IT department?
To learn more about the services we provide, visit
www.serviceassurance.net.

To Contact Mark Directly
By Email: mark@sacorp.net
By Phone: 901-202-5150
By U.S. Mail: 6935 Appling Farms Parkway
                     Suite 109
                     Memphis, TN 38133

Mark is also available to speak for events.

To order copies of The Tallest Pygmy directly, please visit
thetallestpygmy.com. Bulk copies are available at a discount.

For more information, contact Megan Majors at
megan@thetallestpygmy.com or 901-202-5109.